This is Not the End of the Book

Also available in English by Jean-Claude Carrière

Please Mr Einstein

Also available in English by Umberto Eco

Baudolino
The Island of the Day Before
Foucault's Pendulum
The Name of the Rose
Five Moral Pieces
Kant and the Platypus
Serendipities
How to Travel with a Salmon
Travels in Hyperreality
On Beauty
On Ugliness
The Book of Lists

Also written together (with Stephen Jay Gould and Jean-Philippe de Tonnac)

Conversations About the End of Time.

JEAN-CLAUDE CARRIÈRE
& UMBERTO ECO

This is Not the End of the Book

A conversation curated by
Jean-Philippe de Tonnac

Translated from the French by
Polly McLean

HARVILL SECKER · LONDON

Published by Harvill Secker 2011

2 4 6 8 10 9 7 5 3

Copyright © Éditions Grasset & Fasquelle 2009
English translation copyright © Polly McLean 2011

Jean-Claude Carrière and Umberto Eco have asserted their right under the Copyright,
Designs and Patents Act 1988 to be identified as the authors of this work

First published with the title *Ne pensez pas vous débarrasser des livres* in 2009
By Éditions Grasset & Fasquelle

First published in Great Britain in 2011 by
HARVILL SECKER
Random House
20 Vauxhall Bridge Road
London SW1V 2SA

www.randomhouse.co.uk

Addresses for companies within The Random House Group Limited can be found at:
www.randomhouse.co.uk/offices.htm

The Random House Group Limited Reg. No. 954009

A CIP catalogue record for this book is available from the British Library

ISBN 9781846554513

This book is supported by the French Ministry of Foreign Affairs as part of the Burgess
programme run by the Cultural Department of the French Embassy in London.
(www.frenchbooknews.com)

Liberté · Égalité · Fraternité
RÉPUBLIQUE FRANÇAISE

Ouvrage publié avec le soutien du Centre national du livre –
ministère français chargé de la culture

This book is published with support from the French Ministry of Culture –
Centre National du Livre

The Random House Group Limited supports The Forest Stewardship
Council (FSC), the leading international forest certification organisation. All our titles that
are printed on Greenpeace approved FSC certified paper carry the FSC logo. Our paper
procurement policy can be found at www.randomhouse.co.uk/environment

Text designed by Christopher Wakeling
Typeset by Palimpsest Book Production Limited, Falkirk, Stirlingshire
Printed and bound in Germany by GGP Media GmbH

Contents

Preface

In *The Hunchback of Notre-Dame*, Victor Hugo puts these famous words into the mouth of Archdeacon Claude Frollo: 'The book will kill the building . . . When you compare [architecture] to the idea, which . . . needs only a sheet of paper, some ink and a pen, is it surprising that the human intellect should have deserted architecture for the printing press?'

Well, the great cathedrals – those 'bibles in stone' – did not vanish, but the avalanche of manuscripts and then printed text that appeared at the end of the Middle Ages did render them less important. As culture changed, architecture lost its emblematic role. So it is with the book. There is no need to suppose that the electronic book will replace the printed version. Has film killed painting? Television cinema? However, there is no doubt that the book is in the throes of a technological revolution that is changing our relationship to it profoundly.

This extended conversation between Jean-Claude Carrière and Umberto Eco, which took place over the course of several sessions at their two homes, did not begin as an attempt to make emphatic pronouncements about the effects of the widespread (or otherwise) adoption of the electronic book. It was intended, rather, as a discussion about the nature of the book itself. The two men's experience as collectors of rare and ancient books has led them to argue here that the book represents a sort of unsurpassable perfection in the realm of the imagination. Whether we prefer to consider the invention of the book as dating from the first codices (about the eleventh century BC) or from the more ancient papyrus scrolls, it is a tool that has remained remarkably true to itself for a very long time, over and above the changes in its form.

But what is a book? And what will change if we read onscreen rather than by turning the pages of a physical object? What will we gain and, more importantly, what will we lose? Old-fashioned habits, perhaps. A certain sense of the sacred that has surrounded the book in a civilisation that has made it our holy of holies. A peculiar intimacy between the author and reader, which the concept of hypertextuality is bound to damage. A sense of existing in a self-contained world that the book and, along with it, certain ways of reading used to represent.

Carrière and Eco also discuss the mirror that books hold up to humanity. Let's say we consider only the cream of the crop, the masterpieces around which cultural consensus has been built. Is this concentration on 'the best' faithful to the true function of books, which is simply to safeguard the things that forgetfulness constantly threatens to destroy? Shouldn't we accept a less flattering self-image, by considering also the widespread mediocrity conveyed by the written word? Do books necessarily represent the progress that supposedly helps us forget the shadows we always think we have left behind? And, in any case, how can we know that the books that have survived are a true reflection of what human creativity has produced? It's a disturbing question. One can't help remembering all the fires in which so many books have burned and continue to burn. The history of book production is thus indivisible from the history of a real and continuing bibliocaust. Not only accidental fire, but censure, ignorance, stupidity, inquisition, auto-da-fé, negligence and distraction have all been (sometimes fatal) stumbling blocks in the journey of the book. Our ancestors' efforts at archiving and conservation have been unable to prevent the permanent loss of unknown *Divine Comedies*.

One thing is certain: what we call culture is in fact a lengthy process of selection and filtering. So, are the books that remain the best of the huge legacy of centuries gone by? Or the worst? Have we retained the gold nuggets or the mud in the various spheres of creative expression? We still read Euripides, Sophocles and Aeschylus, and think of them as the three great tragic poets of ancient Greece. But Aristotle mentions none of them when he cites the most illustrious tragic writers in his *Poetics*. Were the lost plays better, more representative of Greek theatre? How can we not wonder? Contemporary civilisation, armed with every conceivable kind of technology, is still attempting to conserve culture safely, without much lasting success. However determined we are to learn from the past, our libraries, museums and film archives will only ever contain the works that time has not destroyed. Now more than ever, we realise that culture is made up of what remains after everything else has been forgotten.

But perhaps the most enjoyable part of this conversation is the homage the two men pay to stupidity. This is the crux of the connection between Carrière and Eco – the scriptwriter and the semiologist. Eco has built up a collection of extremely rare books on human error and fakery because, according to him, understanding these qualities is fundamental to any attempt to create a theory of truth. 'The human being is a truly remarkable creature,' he tells us. 'He has discovered fire, built cities, written magnificent poems, interpreted the world, invented mythologies, etc. But at the same time he has never ceased waging war on his fellow humans, being totally wrong, destroying his environment, etc. This mixture of great intellectual powers and base idiocy creates an approximately neutral outcome. So when we decide to explore human stupidity, we are somehow paying tribute to this creature who is part genius, part fool.' If we understand books as reflecting the human striving for self-improvement and transcendence, then we see that of course they express not only our great integrity, but also our terrible baseness. Error is a human characteristic in so far as it belongs only to those who seek and are mistaken. For every solved equation, every proven hypothesis, every shared vision, there have been many journeys that have led nowhere.

Jean-Claude Carrière is just as enthusiastic about what

stupidity can tell us, and has written a much-reprinted dictionary of stupidity. In the course of his conversation with Eco, these two amused observers and chroniclers of the hiccups of history ad-lib effervescently about the flops, gaps, lapses, oversights and irreversible losses that are as much a part of the past as the masterpieces. Their insights into the good and bad fortunes of the book enable us to keep in perspective the predicted changes brought about by the worldwide digitisation of writing and the adoption of new electronic reading tools. They are a humorous tribute to Gutenberg's galaxy that will enchant all readers and book lovers. Who knows – they may even make e-book fans feel nostalgic.

JEAN-PHILIPPE DE TONNAC

The book will never die

Jean-Claude Carrière | At the World Economic Forum in Davos in 2008, one of the speakers was a futurologist who argued that four phenomena would drastically change humanity over the next fifteen years. The first was oil at 500 dollars a barrel. The second was that water, like oil, would become a commercial product, and be traded on the Stock Market. The third was the inevitability of Africa becoming an economic power – certainly something we would all like to see.

The fourth phenomenon, according to this professional prophet, was the disappearance of the book.

The question is whether the permanent eclipse of the book – should it in fact take place – would have the same consequences for humanity as the predicted shortage of water, or affordable oil.

Umberto Eco | Will the book disappear as a result of the Internet? I wrote about this at the time – by which I mean at a time when the question seemed topical. Now, when I'm asked for my opinion, I simply repeat myself, rewriting the same text. Nobody notices this, firstly because there's nothing more original than what has already been said, and secondly because the public (or the journalistic profession at least) is still obsessed

3

with the idea that the book is about to disappear (or perhaps journalists just think their readers are obsessed); therefore, journalists never tire of asking this same question.

There is actually very little to say on the subject. The Internet has returned us to the alphabet. If we thought we had become a purely visual civilisation, the computer returns us to Gutenberg's galaxy; from now on, everyone has to read. In order to read, you need a medium. This medium cannot simply be a computer screen. Spend two hours reading a novel on your computer and your eyes turn into tennis balls. At home, I use a pair of Polaroid glasses to protect my eyes from the ill effects of unbroken onscreen reading. And in any case, the computer depends on electricity and cannot be read in a bath, or even lying on your side in bed.

One of two things will happen: either the book will continue to be the medium for reading, or its replacement will resemble what the book has always been, even before the invention of the printing press. Alterations to the book-as-object have modified neither its function nor its grammar for more than 500 years. The book is like the spoon, scissors, the hammer, the wheel. Once invented, it cannot be improved. You cannot make a spoon that is better than a spoon. When designers try to improve on something like the corkscrew, their success is very limited; most of their 'improvements' don't even work. Philippe Starck attempted an innovative lemon-squeezer; his version may be very handsome, but it lets the pips through. The book has been thoroughly tested, and it's very hard to see how it could be improved on for its current purposes. Perhaps it will evolve in terms of components; perhaps the pages will no longer be made of paper. But it will still be the same thing.

J.-C. C. | It seems that the latest versions of the e-book have put it in direct competition with the printed book.

U. E. | There's no doubt that a lawyer could take his 25,000 case documents home more easily if they were loaded onto an e-book. In many areas, the electronic book will turn out to be remarkably convenient. But I am still not convinced – even with first-rate reading technology – that it would be particularly advisable to read *War and Peace* on an e-book. We shall see. It's certainly true that we won't be able to read our editions of Tolstoy for ever, or indeed any of the books in our collection that are printed on wood pulp, because they are starting to decompose. The Gallimard and Vrin editions from the 1950s are mostly gone already. I can no longer even pick up my copy of Étienne Gilson's *The Spirit of Medieval Philosophy*, which served me so well when I

5

was writing my thesis. The pages literally fall to pieces. I could of course buy a new edition, but I'm attached to the old one, with its different-coloured annotations telling the story of my different readings.

Jean-Philippe de Tonnac | Why not concede that with the development of new media better and better adapted to the demands of e-reading – whether of encyclopaedias or novels – there will be a slow loss of interest in the object of the book in its traditional form?

U. E. | Anything might happen. In future books may interest only a handful of ardent enthusiasts, who will satisfy their backward-looking curiosity in museums and libraries.

J.-C. C. | If there are any left.

U. E. | But one can also imagine that the fantastic invention that is the Internet may likewise disappear. Just as airships have disappeared from our skies. The future of the airship collapsed when *The Hindenburg* caught fire in New York State just before the war. The same goes for Concorde: the Gonesse accident in 2000 was fatal. Now that's a very interesting story. An aeroplane was invented that could cross the Atlantic in three hours instead of eight. Who could argue with such progress? But after the Gonesse disaster, Concorde was deemed too expensive and abandoned. What kind of reason is that? The atomic bomb is very expensive too.

J.-P. DE T. | Hermann Hesse had some interesting things to say about the 're-legitimisation' of the book that he thought would result from technical developments. He was writing in the 1950s: 'The more the need for entertainment and mainstream education can be met by new inventions, the more the book will recover its dignity and authority. We have not yet quite reached the point where young competitors, such as radio, cinema, etc., have taken over functions from the book that it can't afford to lose.'

J.-C. C. | In that regard he wasn't mistaken. Cinema, radio and even television have taken nothing from the book – nothing that it couldn't afford to lose.

U. E. | At a certain point in time, man invented the written word. We can think of writing as an extension of the hand, and therefore as almost biological. It is the communication tool most closely linked to the body. Once invented, it could never be given up. As I said about the book, it was like the invention of the wheel. Today's wheels

7

are the same as wheels in prehistoric times. Our modern inventions – cinema, radio, Internet – are not biological.

J.-C. C. | You're right to draw attention to this: we have never needed to read and write as much as we do today. If you can't read and write, then you can't use a computer. And you have to be able to read and write in a more complex way than ever before, because we have invented new characters and symbols. Our alphabet has expanded. It is becoming harder and harder to learn to read. If our computers were able to transcribe speech with precision, then we would experience a return to oral culture. Which brings us to another question: is it possible to express oneself well if one cannot read or write?

U. E. | Homer, of course, would say yes.

J.-C. C. | But Homer belonged to an oral tradition. He acquired his learning by way of that tradition, before anything in Greece was written down. Can we imagine a contemporary author dictating his novel without writing it down, and knowing nothing of the body of literature that has preceded him? His novel might be charming, naïve, fresh, unusual. But it does seem to me that it would lack what one might, for want of a better word, call culture. Rimbaud wrote his superb poetry when he was very young. But he was far from being an autodidact. At the age of sixteen, he had already benefited from a solid classical education. He could write Latin verse.

There is nothing more ephemeral
than long-term media formats

J.-P. DE T. | We are pondering the durability of books in an era when the prevailing culture seems to be tending towards other, perhaps more high-performing tools. But what about the media formats that were supposed to provide durable storage for our data and personal memories? I'm thinking of the floppy disks, video-tapes and CD-ROMs that we have already left behind.

J.-C. C. | In 1985, the French Culture Minister Jack Lang asked me to set up and run a national cinema and televi-sion school, La Fémis. I put together a great technical team under the direction of Jack Gajos, and chaired the organisation from 1986 to 1996. Obviously, for those ten years, I had to be completely up to speed on every innovation in our field.

One of our main challenges was simply showing films to our students. When studying and analysing a film, you have to be able to stop, rewind, pause, and sometimes proceed one shot at a time. With the tradi-tional reel this cannot be done. At the time we had videotapes, but they wore out very quickly and were completely useless after three or four years. It was around that time that the Vidéothèque de Paris was set up to conserve every piece of film and photography about Paris. The Vidéothèque had to choose between archiving these images on videotape or on CD – both at the time known as 'long-term media formats'. It chose to invest in video. Other people were trying out floppy disks, which were getting the hard sell. Two or three years later, the CD-ROM appeared in California. At last, we had the answer. We watched demonstration after thrilling demonstration. I remember the first CD-ROM we saw. It was about Egypt. We were staggered, and completely sold on it. We bowed low before this new invention, which seemed to solve all the difficulties we had been struggling with for years. And yet the American factories that used to make those little marvels closed down more than seven years ago.

On the other hand, our mobile phones, iPods, etc. are capable of ever-greater feats. We're told that the Japanese write and publish their novels on them. The Internet has become portable and wireless. There is also the promise of Video on Demand, folding screens and all sorts of other phenomena. Who knows?

It may seem as if I'm talking about things that changed over a very long time-span, a matter of centuries. But all this has taken place in barely twenty years. It doesn't take long to forget. Less and less long, perhaps. These thoughts are probably rather commonplace, but it's important not to throw out commonplace things. At the start of a journey, in any case.

U. E. | A few years ago, a CD-ROM of Jacques-Paul Migne's 221-volume *Patrologia Latina* was on the market for 50,000 dollars. As a result, only big libraries could buy the *Patrologia*, not poor scholars (having said that, we medievalists soon started gleefully copying them). These days, all you have to do is subscribe and you can consult the *Patrologia* online. The same goes for Diderot's *Encyclopédie*, which was formerly sold by the dictionary publisher Robert on CD-ROM. Today, I can search it online for nothing.

J.-C. C. | When the DVD came on the market, we were sure that we had finally acquired the perfect solution – a format that would permanently resolve all our requirements around data storage and group screenings. Until then I had never created a personal film library. When DVDs came along, I was finally sure that I had my 'lasting media format'. How wrong could I be? They are now announcing much smaller disks, which require new players and, like the e-book, can hold a substantial number of films. Even our good old DVDs will be given the push – unless we keep the old players that allow us to watch them.

There's actually a trend for collecting things that technology is ruthlessly outdating. A Belgian film-maker friend of mine keeps eighteen computers in his cellar, just so that he can watch old work. Which goes to show that there is nothing more ephemeral than long-term media formats. Enthusiastic collectors of incunabula, such as you and I, are probably quite tickled by these banal, now rather hackneyed musings on the frailty of contemporary media formats. Look at this. This little incunabulum comes from my bookshelves. It was written in Latin and printed in Paris at the end of the fifteenth century. On the final page the following is printed in French: 'These hours for the use of Rome were completed on the twenty-seventh day of September year one thousand four hundred and ninety-eight for Jean Poitevin, bookseller, of rue Neuve-Notre-Dame, Paris.' Though the word 'use' has been spelled in an old-fashioned way, and this manner of describing the date and year has long been abandoned, we can still decipher the text easily enough. And so we can still read a text printed five centuries ago. But you can no longer read, or rather watch, a video or CD-ROM that is only a few years old. Unless you have space for a lot of old computers in your basement.

J.-P. DE T. | It's important to emphasise the increasing pace with which these new formats are becoming obsolete, forcing us to reorganise our working methods, our back-up systems, the very way we think . . .

U. E. | And this increasing speed is contributing to the loss of our cultural heritage. That is definitely one of the thorniest issues of our time. On the one hand, we invent all kinds of tools to preserve our memories, all kinds of recording equipment, and ways in which to transport knowledge. This is certainly major progress in comparison to the days when you had to rely on mnemonics to remember – people had to rely on their own memories, because they didn't have everything they needed to know at their fingertips. On the other hand, we have to acknowledge that, above and beyond the perishable nature of these tools, which is in itself a problem, we are not even-handed with the cultural objects that we choose to preserve. For example, if you want to buy an original of one of the great comic strips, it is horribly expensive, because they are so rare (these days, a single page of Alex Raymond's work costs a fortune). But why are they so rare? Simply because the newspapers that used to publish them threw the plates in the bin the moment the strip had been printed.

J.-P. DET. | What were the mnemonics that people used before the invention of artificial memories such as books and hard drives?

J.-C. C. | Take the case of Alexander the Great. He is once again about to make a far-reaching decision, and has been told of a woman who can predict the future with total accuracy. He summons this woman, to teach him her art. She tells him that he must light a big fire and read the future in the smoke from the fire, as from a book. But she gives the warrior one warning. While reading the smoke, he must on no account think of the left eye of a crocodile. The right eye if he must, but never the left.

Alexander gave up on knowing the future. Why? Because as soon as you have been instructed not to think of something, you can think of nothing else. The prohibition becomes an obligation. It is in fact impossible not to think of that crocodile's left eye. The beast's eye has taken over your memory, and your mind.

Sometimes, as in Alexander's case, remembering and not being able to forget is a problem, a tragedy even. Some people have the ability to remember everything, using very simple mnemonics; they are called mnemonists, and have been studied by the Russian neurologist Alexander Luria. Peter Brook based his play *I Am a Phenomenon* on one of Luria's books. If you tell a mnemonist something, he will be unable to forget it. He is like a perfect but crazed machine, recording everything without discrimination. Which is actually a flaw, rather than a quality.

U. E. | All mnemonic techniques use the image of a city or palace in which each area or place is linked to the thing that must be remembered. In his *De oratore*, Cicero describes Simonides attending a dinner with many of Greece's senior dignitaries. At a certain point in the evening, Simonides takes a break from the gathering, only for the ceiling to collapse and all the other guests to be killed. Simonides is called in to identify the bodies. He manages to do this by remembering each person's place at the table.

The art of mnemonics is thus to associate spatial imagery with objects or concepts in order to link them. The reason that Alexander can no longer behave freely is that he has linked the crocodile's left eye to the smoke he must read. The memorising arts were still practised in the Middle Ages, but it seems that they were gradually lost with the invention of the printing press. Paradoxically, that was when the great books on mnemonic techniques were published.

J.-C. C. | You mentioned the original plates of the great comic strips being thrown in the bin after publication. The same thing happened with cinema, and many films were lost for ever. It was only in the 1920s and '30s that cinema became, in Europe, the 'seventh art'. After that it was considered worth conserving films, because they belonged to the history of art. And so they created the first film archives, in Russia and then in France. The Americans, however, don't consider cinema an art. For them it is a renewable product. They are constantly remaking *Zorro*, or *Nosferatu*, or *Tarzan*, and because the previous version might be a rival to the new one – especially if the old film was good – they throw away the old film stock. In fact, the American film archive wasn't created until the 1970s! It was a real struggle to raise finance, to convince the Americans of the importance of their own cinematic history. The world's first film school was likewise in Russia. We owe it to Eisenstein, who thought it crucial to create a film school as good as the best schools of painting and architecture.

U. E. | In Italy, great poets like Gabriele d'Annunzio were already writing for the cinema at the beginning of the twentieth century. D'Annunzio co-wrote the script for *Cabiria* with Giovanni Pastrone. In America, that would have been bad for his reputation.

J.-C. C. | All this is even more the case with TV. Creating

20

television archives seemed absurd at the outset. There was a radical change of perspective with the creation of the INA (France's National Audiovisual Institute) to preserve audiovisual archives.

U.E. | I did some work in television in 1954, and I remember that everything was screened live, and they weren't yet using magnetic tape recording. To make a recording, they used a method they called 'Transcriber', until they realised the word wasn't actually used in English-speaking TV. It was simply a camera that filmed the screen. But it was so tedious and expensive to use that they didn't bring it out much, and lots of programmes were lost.

J.-C.C. | I know a lovely example of this. A televisual incunabulum, if you like. In 1951 or '52, Peter Brook shot *King Lear* for American TV with Orson Welles in the title role. The programmes were broadcast without being recorded in any way, and nothing was kept. But as it turned out, a film did in fact exist. Someone had happened to film the television screen during the broadcast of the programme. This film is now a prize exhibit in New York's Museum of Television and Radio. In many ways that story reminds me of the history of the book.

U. E. | Up to a point. The idea of collecting books goes back a very long way, so what took place in the film world never happened with books. The cult of the written page, and later of the book, goes back as far as writing itself. Even the Romans wanted to own and collect scrolls. The books we have lost have been lost for other reasons. They have been destroyed through religious censorship and because libraries, rather like cathedrals, had a great tendency to burn down at the slightest provocation, chiefly because both were built mainly of wood. In medieval times, a cathedral or library burning down was a bit like a plane being shot down during the Pacific War. Normal. The fact that the library in *The Name of the Rose* ends up burning down would not at the time have been particularly out of the ordinary.

Indeed, the fact that books were liable to be destroyed by fire was the reason people wanted to keep them safe, and collected them. This is the very basis of monasticism. The repeated barbarian invasions of Rome, and their habit of setting fire to the city before they left, seem to have led the Romans to seek out a safe place for their books. And what safer place than a monastery to put books out of reach of the dangers that threatened the preservation of their history? At the same time, this practice inevitably entailed saving certain books at the expense of others, and so the filtering process was begun.

J.-C. C. | The cult of rare films, on the other hand, is only just beginning. There are even people who collect film scripts. In the old days the script would go in the bin as soon as the film had been shot – like those comic-strip plates you were talking about. But then, in the 1940s, people started to wonder whether the script might not retain a certain value of its own, once the film had been made. A commercial value, at least.

U. E. | And now there's a kind of cult around famous scripts, like the script for *Casablanca*.

J.-C. C. | Especially, of course, if the script has been annotated by the director. In some circles Fritz Lang's annotated film scripts are worshipped, almost fetishised, as collectors' objects. Others have been beautifully bound by their owners. But let me return to my earlier comment for a moment, about creating a personal film archive. Which format is best? Storing traditional reels at home would be impossible. You'd need a projection room, a special viewing room and lots of storage space. As we know, videotapes lose colour and definition and wear out fast. CD-ROMs are over. DVDs won't last long. And in any case, we can't count on always having access to enough energy to run all these machines. What if the July 2006 New York power cut had spread, and continued? Lose electricity and you lose everything, for ever. But even if our entire audio-visual legacy were to be lost in a power cut, we would still be able to read books in the light from the sun, or in the evening by candlelight. The twentieth century is the first century to give future generations moving pictures of itself, of its own history, along with sound recordings – although on formats that remain inse-cure. It's strange to think that we have no sounds of the past. We can of course presume that birdsong was the same, the sound of a running stream . . .

U. E. | But not human voices. Museum collections show us that our ancestors' beds were smaller than ours – and so the people must have been shorter, too. This in turn means that their intonation and the quality of their voices would have been different. When I listen to an old Caruso recording, I always wonder whether the difference between his voice and that of today's great tenors is due exclusively to the technical quality of the recording and the media format, or whether human voices at the beginning of the twentieth century were in fact different from ours. There are decades of increased protein intake and medical advances between the voices of Caruso and Pavarotti. Italian immigrants

24

to the United States at the beginning of the twentieth century tended to measure about five foot three, whereas their grandsons average five eleven.

J.-C.C. | When I was running the French film school, I challenged the student sound engineers to re-create certain sounds and sonic atmospheres of the past. For example, I asked them to create a soundtrack for Boileau's satirical poem 'Les Embarras de Paris'. I reminded them that the road surfaces were made of wood, the horse-drawn carriages had iron wheels, the houses were not as high, etc.

The poem starts like this: '*Qui frappe l'air bon Dieu de ces lugubres cris?*' ('Who, by God, strikes the air with dismal cries?'). What would be the nature of a 'dismal' cry in seventeenth-century night-time Paris? This attempt to dive into times past by way of sound is fascinating, but difficult. How can one ever be sure?

All this is to say that, even if visual and sound recordings of the twentieth century are wiped out by a gigantic electricity failure, or for some other reason, we will always have the book. We will always find ways of teaching a child to read. The idea of culture being on the road to ruin, of memories being endangered, is of course as old as the hills. Probably older than the written object itself. Let me give you an example from Persian history. We know that contemporary

Afghanistan was one of the cradles of Persian culture. When the Mongol threat – and the Mongols tended to destroy everything in their path – started to intensify during the eleventh and twelfth centuries, there was an exodus of intellectuals and artists living in, for example, Balkh, among them the father of the yet-to-be-born Rumi. They took their most precious manuscripts with them and travelled westwards, towards Turkey. (Like many exiled Persians, Rumi lived his whole life at Konya, in Anatolia.) There's a story of one of these fugitives, reduced to great poverty on the road to exile, using the precious books he has brought with him as pillows. Books that today would be worth a small fortune. (In Tehran, an antiquarian bookseller once tried to sell me an extraordinary collection of ancient illustrated manuscripts.) So we can see that all the great civilisations asked themselves the same question: what to do with a culture under threat? How to save it? And what to save?

U.E. | And when an evacuation does take place, when people do have time to carry the emblems of their civilisation to safety, it is easier to save scrolls, codices, incunabula and books than sculpture or paintings.

J.-C. C. | And yet what about the mysterious disappearance of all the volumina, the scrolls of Roman Antiquity?

It is known that Roman noblemen kept libraries of thousands of works. A few volumina can be consulted at the Vatican Library, but most have not survived to our day. The oldest fragment of a Gospel manuscript that we have been able to find dates from the fourth century. I remember seeing a manuscript of Virgil's *Georgics* from the fourth or fifth century at the Vatican. Wonderful! The top half of each page was illustration. But I have never in my life seen a complete volumen. The most ancient pieces of writing I have ever seen were the manuscripts from the Dead Sea, in a museum in Jerusalem. They had been preserved thanks to utterly unique climatic conditions. The same goes for the Egyptian papyrus scrolls, which I think are the oldest of all.

J. P. DE T. | You mention papyrus and perhaps paper as the media for these writings. But surely we must also look at older media, which in some way also belong to the history of the book . . .

J.-C. C. | Of course. The media used for writing have been many – stelae, tablets, cloth. And there are many different types of writing. But more interesting than the media used is the message that these fragments have brought to us from a past we can hardly imagine.

I'd like to show you an image from an auction catalogue that I received just this morning. It's a footprint of the Buddha. Let's imagine the scenario. The Buddha is walking, slowly advancing through his story. One of the Buddha's physical characteristics is that he has messages written on the soles of his feet. These messages are of course fundamental. When he walks, the Buddha makes an impression on the ground, as if each of his footsteps were a printing block.

U. E. | An ancient Hollywood Boulevard.

J.-C. C. | If you like. As the Buddha walks, he teaches. You simply read his footsteps. And, of course, this printing block is not just any old printing block. It contains the whole of Buddhist teaching, in other words the 108 precepts that represent all the animate and inanimate worlds encompassed by the Buddha's wisdom.

But this footprint also features other images: stupas, little temples, wheels of life, animals, trees, water, light, nagas, offerings – all of it contained within a single footprint. Printing before printing existed. A symbolic imprint.

J. P. DE T. | So many footprints, so many messages for disciples to decode. Surely we must link our exploration of the origins of writing to a study of the creation of our sacred texts? Because it was upon these documents, created according to a logic we find hard to understand, that the great faith movements were built. But on what foundations, exactly? What value should we give to these footprints or to our 'four' Gospels, for example? Why four? And why those four?

J.-C. C. | Why four, indeed, when many more existed? Even after a council of churchmen had selected those four Gospels, new testimonies continued to be found. They only found the Gospel according to Thomas – older than those of Matthew, Mark, Luke and John, and a verbatim account of the words of Jesus – in the twentieth century.

Most specialists today agree that there was also an original Gospel, known as the Q Gospel – the source Gospel, from the German *Quelle* – which could perhaps be pieced together from the Gospels of Luke, Matthew and John, each of which refers to the same source. This original Gospel has completely disappeared. And yet experts have been attempting to reconstruct it from what they can deduce of its existence.

What then is a sacred text? An enigma, a riddle? In the case of Buddhism, things were a little different. Like Jesus, Buddha didn't write anything down. But he gave teachings over a much longer period than

Jesus. They think that Jesus preached for two or three years at most. The Buddha taught for at least thirty-five. Immediately after the Buddha's death, his close disciple Ananda started writing down his words, helped by the group who had surrounded him. The Buddha's first teaching, the Sermon at Benares – containing the 'Four Noble Truths', learned by heart and carefully transcribed, and still the basic teaching of all Buddhist schools – is no longer than a single page of writing. At the outset, Buddhism was a single page. And this single page has gone on, starting with Ananda's re-transcriptions, to beget millions of books.

J. P. DE T. | A single conserved page. But perhaps all the others have simply disappeared. How can one know? Faith is what lends this text its special value. But perhaps the Buddha's real teachings were contained in his footprints, or in documents that have been lost or destroyed?

J.-C. C. | Let's pose ourselves a classic dilemma: the world is under threat, and we can only safeguard a few cultural objects. Civilisation might be wiped out, perhaps by a massive environmental catastrophe. We have to act fast. We cannot protect or save everything. So what would we choose? And in which media?

U. E. | We have already talked about how modern media formats quickly become obsolete. Why run the risk of choosing objects that may become mute and indecipherable? It is proven that books are superior to every other object that our cultural industries have put on the market in recent years. So, wanting to choose something easily transportable and that has shown itself equal to the ravages of time, I choose the book.

J.-C. C. | Since we've been comparing the way modern media formats fit into our busy lives with the whole history of the book, including its manufacture and dissemination, I would like to give you an example of a book that managed to be closely linked to the passage of history, more bent to its rhythms. The eighteenth-century writer Restif de la Bretonne wrote *The Nights of Paris* by noting down what he saw during his nocturnal rambles through the city. Did he really witness these things? Critics disagree. Restif was known as a fantasist, who might easily have imagined the world he was representing as real. For example, every time he sleeps with a whore, he discovers that she is one of his daughters.

The final two volumes of *The Nights of Paris* were written during the Revolution. Each night Restif not only gathered the material for his story, but wrote it down and printed it in the morning, on a basement printing press. And because, during this troubled time, he couldn't get hold of paper, he collected posters, bills and leaflets during his nocturnal wanderings, and boiled them up to create a poor-quality pulp. The paper used for the final two volumes was completely different from that of the earlier ones. Another characteristic of Restif's work is that he was so short of time that he used abbreviations. For example, he wrote 'Rev.' instead of 'Revolution'. It's very striking. The book itself is testament to the haste of a man who wishes to communicate events at all costs, to match the pace of history. And if the facts he recounts are not true, then Restif must have been a phenomenal liar. For example, he describes seeing a character he calls 'the groper'. This man slinks through the crowd surrounding the guillotine, groping a woman's buttocks every time a head falls.

It was Restif who described transvestites – at the time called 'effeminates' – under the Revolution. He also evokes a scene that Milos Forman and I went crazy about. Several prisoners are brought to the scaffold in a cart. One man's little dog has followed him. Before stepping up to his execution, the man turns to the crowd and asks for someone to take care of his dog. It is very affectionate, he adds. He is holding it in his arms, trying to give it away. The crowd insults him. The guards grow impatient, snatch the dog from the prisoner's hands and drop the guillotine. The whimpering dog licks his master's blood from the tray. The exasperated guards stab the dog to death, only for the crowd to turn against them: 'Murderers! Shame on you! What did that poor dog ever do to you?'

I've deviated slightly from the point, but what Restif was trying to create – a book as report, a 'live book' – seems to me unique. Now let us return to the question at hand: which books would we attempt to save in the event of a disaster? Your house is on fire – what would you save first?

U. E. | Having spoken so passionately in favour of books, I had better admit that the first thing I would save is my 250-gigabyte hard drive, which contains all my writing from the last thirty years. After that, if there were still time, I would of course try to save one of my oldest books – not necessarily the most valuable, but the one I love the most. But how to choose? I am extremely attached to lots of them. I would hope not to have too long to deliberate. Perhaps I would take Bernhard von Breydenbach's *Peregrinatio in Terram Sanctam*, Spier, Drach, 1490, on account of its wonderful illustrated plates on several folded pages.

J.-C. C. | For my part, I would definitely take an Alfred Jarry manuscript, as well as one by André Breton, and a book by Lewis Carroll that contains a letter he wrote.

A terrible thing happened to Octavio Paz. His library burned down. Now that really was a disaster. Just imagine the library of Octavio Paz – it contained signed copies of books from Surrealists the world over. It was the great tragedy of his final two years.

If I were asked the same question in relation to film, I would find it much harder to choose. Why? For the reason we discussed before – so many films have disappeared. Even some of the films I've worked on myself will never be seen again. Once the negative has been lost, the film no longer exists. And even if the negative does still exist, finding it is often a huge undertaking, and making a copy extremely expensive.

It seems to me that the world of the image, and in particular of film, illustrates perfectly the challenges posed by the exponential acceleration in media formats. You and I were born in the first century in history to invent new languages in this regard. If we were discussing all this 120 years ago, we would only have been able to talk about theatre and the book. Radio, cinema, sound and voice recordings, television, 3-D films and comic strips would not have existed. And each time that a new medium appears, it has to prove that it isn't subject to the rules and constraints that have shaped every previous invention. The new medium proudly considers itself unique. As if it automatically brings with it a natural ability on the part of its new users that will spare them the need to learn how to use it. An intrinsic talent. As if it can sweep aside everything that has preceded it, suddenly rendering illiterate and backward anyone who dares reject it.

I have witnessed this ruse all my life. The truth is very different. Each new medium requires a long learning process, all the longer because our brains have been moulded by the languages that preceded it. The years 1903–5 saw the birth of a new cinematic language. Many novelists thought they would be able to go from writing novels to writing screenplays just like that. But they were wrong. They did not realise that these two written objects – the novel and the screenplay – actually necessitated two different types of writing.

Using new media formats is nothing to do with aptitude. It's something you have to learn. Adapting a play for radio is incredibly difficult.

It took chickens almost a
century to learn not to cross
the road

J.-P. DE T. | Let's come back to the changes in technology that may or may not persuade us to leave the book behind. Today's media formats are definitely more fragile and less long-lasting than our wonderfully tenacious incunabula. And yet, whether we like it or not, these new tools are having a profound effect on our thought patterns, and gradually altering them from those engendered by the book.

U. E. | The speed with which technology reinvents itself has forced us into an unsustainably frequent reorganisation of our mental habits. We feel the need to buy a new computer every couple of years, precisely because they are designed to become obsolete after a certain time, and to be more expensive to repair than to replace. We feel the need to buy a new car every year, because the new model is always better in terms of security features, gadgets, etc. And every new piece of technology requires the acquisition of a new system of reflexes, which in turn requires effort on our part, and all of this on a shorter and shorter cycle. It took chickens almost a century to learn not to cross the road. In the end, the species did adapt to the new traffic conditions. But we don't have that kind of time.

J.-C. C. | But is it even possible to adapt to a rhythm that is accelerating to this pointless degree? Take the example of film editing. Music videos have increased the pace of editing to such an extent that it simply can't go any faster. You wouldn't be able to see the images. I give this example to show how a cycle is created in which a media format gives birth to its own language, which in turn forces the format to evolve, and so on, in ever more hasty and hurried circles. In today's Hollywood 'action' films, no shot lasts more than three seconds. It has become a kind of rule. A man goes home, opens the door, hangs up his coat and goes upstairs. Nothing happens, he isn't under any threat, and yet the sequence is cut into eighteen shots. As if the technology is dictating the action, as if the action were in the camera itself, rather than in what it depicts.

At the outset, the techniques of film-making were simple. You set up a fixed camera and filmed a theatrical scene. Actors entered, did what they had to do and left. Then people realised that by putting a camera on a moving train, the images sped past on the camera, and therefore on the screen. The camera could possess and reconstruct a movement. It therefore began to move about the studio – cautiously at first, until it gradually became a character in its own right. It turned to the right, and then the left. The two

40

images thus obtained had to be spliced together, and this process of editing gave rise to a new language. Buñuel was born at the same time as cinema, in 1900. He told me that when he went to the movies in Zaragoza in 1907 or 1908, an *explicador* with a long baton would explain what was happening on the screen. The new language was still unintelligible. It had not yet been assimilated. Though we are now used to it, it is still constantly being refined, perfected and – thank God – perverted by great film-makers.

Film, like literature, has a 'noble' language that is intentionally lofty and pompous, an ordinary, banal language and even a slang. It is also the case that, as Proust said of the great authors, great film-makers at least partially invent their own language.

U. E. | The Italian politician Amintore Fanfani was born at the beginning of the last century and so at a time when film was not yet mainstream. He once said in an interview that he didn't often go to the cinema, because he found it hard to comprehend that the character he was seeing filmed from behind was the same character he had seen from the front a moment before.

J.-C. C. | Film-makers had to take considerable care not to lose the audience, who were entering a new realm of artistic comprehension. In classical theatre the action lasts for the same time as its depiction. In Shakespeare and Racine, there are no cuts within scenes. Time is the same on the stage and in the stalls. I think Godard was one of the first, in *Breathless*, to film a two-person scene in a room and edit it down so that the film featured only moments or fragments of that long scene.

U. E. | It seems to me that comic strips had been using an artificial construction of narrative time for a while before that. And yet, as a fan and collector of 1930s comic strips, I find it quite impossible to read contemporary graphic novels, or at least the most avant-garde. But it's important not to bury one's head in the sand. I played my seven-year-old grandson at one of his beloved computer games recently, and lost by 280 to 10. I used to play pinball, and I often spend spare moments fighting intergalactic wars with monsters from outer space on my computer. I'm quite good at it. But in this case I had to concede defeat. That said, even my genius of a grandson may no longer be able to understand the newest technologies when he's twenty. What I'm saying is that there are areas of knowledge in which it is impossible to remain abreast of new developments for very long. A person is only a top researcher in nuclear physics for as long as they can make the effort to understand all the data and keep their head above water. After that they become a teacher, or go into business. The same goes for football players. At a certain age, you become a coach.

J.-C. C. | The publisher Odile Jacob once suggested I talk to Claude Lévi-Strauss about creating a book of conversations between the two of us. He refused with great charm, saying: 'I don't want to repeat what I have already said better.' Wonderfully clear-headed. Even in anthropology, there comes a time when the game – your game, our game – is over. And that was Lévi-Strauss, who lived to be hundred!

U. E. | I can no longer teach, for exactly the same reason. Our uncalled-for longevity mustn't blind us to the fact that the world of knowledge is in constant flux and that of course we can only have a proper handle on it for a limited period of time.

J.-C. C. | How would you explain the adaptive capacities of your grandson, who at age seven is able to master new languages that we, despite all our efforts, fail fully to grasp?

U. E. | Like other children of his age he has been exposed, on a daily basis, since the age of two, to all kinds of stimulation that simply didn't exist when we were young. My son was twenty when I brought home my first computer, in 1983. I showed him my purchase, and offered to explain how it worked. He said he wasn't interested. So I sat down in my corner and got on with exploring my new toy. I had all sorts of difficulties, of course (remember we had to programme in languages like BASIC and Pascal; Windows hadn't yet changed our lives). One day my son, seeing me struggling, came over and said: 'You should do it like this.' And the computer worked.

I supposed he had been using the computer when I was out. But I still couldn't see how he had been able to master it so much faster than me. He must have already had the knack. You and I do certain things automatically – like turning the key to start the car, or turning on a switch. In this case it was a matter of clicking, or pressing, and my son had a head start.

J.-C. C. | To turn or to click – that's rather an instructive comment. When I think of how we read books, our eyes go from left to right and top to bottom. In Arabic, Persian and Hebrew, it's the other way round; the eye travels from right to left. I wonder what impact this has had on camera movements in film. Most tracking shots in Western cinema move from left to right, whereas I have often noticed the opposite in Iranian films, for example. And why shouldn't our reading

44

habits influence our ways of seeing? The instinctive movements of our eyes?

U. E. | In that case we'd need to know whether Western farmers plough their fields from left to right on the way out and right to left on the way back, in contrast to Egyptian or Iranian farmers, who would start from right to left and return left to right. Because ploughing follows the same pattern as boustrophedonic writing. This seems to me important and underexplored. The Nazis would have been able to identify Jewish farmers immediately. But let's get back to the point. We were talking about change and the rate at which it is increasing. But we also said that there are technical innovations that do not change, such as the book. We could add the bicycle, and even spectacles. Not to mention the alphabet. Once perfection has been achieved, it cannot be improved.

J.-C. C. | I'd like to return to cinema, if you don't mind, and its astonishing faithfulness to itself. Cinema is still a rectangle projected onto a flat surface, and has been so for more than a hundred years. It is the ultimate magic lantern. The language has evolved, but the form remains the same. More and more cinemas are gearing up to screen 3-D and also Surround Vision films. Let's just hope it's not all style and no substance.

Can cinema be improved on, in terms of form? Is it young, or old? I don't know the answer. I know that literature is old. That's what I'm told. But perhaps it isn't as old as all that . . . and perhaps we shouldn't play at being Nostradamus here, because our words may soon be proven wrong.

U. E. | Speaking of failed predictions, life once taught me a great lesson. It was in the Sixties and I was working for a publishing house. We were sent a fascinating book by an American sociologist, describing the generations to come and announcing the emergence of a new white-collar generation, with crew-cut hair and no interest whatsoever in politics. We decided to have it translated, but the translation was poor and I spent a long time editing it. In the meantime the Berkeley riots happened, as well as May 1968, and the sociologist's analysis seemed miles wide of the mark. So I threw the manuscript in the bin.

J.-C. C. | We've been rather derisory about the inability of our current media formats to store our memories reliably over the long term. But it seems to me that we are also sorely in need of reliable prophets. That Davos futurologist was deaf and blind to the approaching financial crisis when he predicted a barrel of oil at 500 dollars. And how should he know? Where does he get his X-ray vision? Does he hold a degree in forecasting? Oil increased to 150 dollars a barrel, and then fell back down to just over fifty for no apparent reason. It may climb again, or fall some more. We don't know. The future is not a career.

It's in the nature of true as well as false prophets to be frequently in the wrong. I can't remember who it was that said: 'If the future is the future, it's always unexpected.' The future's main quality is to be consistently surprising. I'm often struck by the fact that not a single author in the great era of science fiction from the start of the twentieth century to the end of the 1950s ever imagined plastic, which has become so ubiquitous in our lives. Fiction, and the future, is always created from our current starting place. But the future isn't a continuation of the present. I could give you a thousand examples of this. In the Sixties, Buñuel and I went to Mexico to work on a script. We were working in a very remote area. I had brought a small portable typewriter with a red and black ribbon. If that ribbon had broken, there was no way I could have replaced it in the local town of Zitácuaro. I think now of how luxurious a computer would have seemed at the time. But we were a million miles from anticipating it.

J.-P. DE T. | This tribute to the book is simply trying to show that contemporary technologies aren't likely to render it obsolete. But perhaps we should also put into perspective the progress that some of these technologies are supposed to have made. I am thinking particularly of Jean-Claude's description of Restif de la Bretonne printing the previous night's adventures at dawn.

J.-C. C. | That was certainly quite a feat. The great Brazilian collector José Mindlin once showed me an edition of *Les Misérables* that was printed and published in Portuguese, in Rio, in 1862 – the same year that it was first published in France. Just two months after Paris! As Hugo wrote the book, his editor Hetzel was sending each chapter to the foreign editors, meaning that *Les Misérables* was disseminated in much the same way as contemporary best-sellers, which come onto the market in several languages and several countries simultaneously. It can be helpful to see our supposed technological triumphs in relation to what has come before. In the case of Victor Hugo, things happened faster then than they do today.

U. E. | In a similar vein, thirty-odd pirate editions made Alessandro Manzoni's 1827 novel *The Betrothed* wildly popular all over the world, without earning him a single penny. Manzoni had wanted to create an illustrated edition with the editor Redaelli de Milan and the engraver Gonin de Turin, and publish it instalment by instalment. But a Neapolitan editor pirated the text on a week-by-week basis, meaning that Manzoni didn't make anything from any of those thirty editions. That's another example of the relativity of our technological wizardry. And there are many more. In the seventeenth century, Robert Fludd used to publish three or four books per year. He lived in England. The books were published in Amsterdam. He would receive the proofs, correct them, check the illustrations and send the whole thing back . . . but how? These were 600-page illustrated books. Their postal system must have been better than ours. And Galileo kept up a correspondence with Johannes Kepler and all the other scholars of his time. He heard about new discoveries almost as soon as they happened.

But perhaps we should balance this eulogy to the old days with the following consideration. In the 1960s, when I was working as an editor, I commissioned a translation of Derek de Solla Price's *Little Science, Big Science*. In it the author uses statistics to show that in the eighteenth century it was feasible for a good scientist to keep abreast of every new development in his field, whereas today it would be inconceivable for that same scientist to read even the abstracts of every relevant article published. And so, despite all our performance-enhancing technology, the modern scholar probably has less time than someone like Robert Fludd to write and edit books.

J.-C. C. | Then there are our USB sticks and other ways of storing and carrying information. These too are nothing new. At the end of the eighteenth century, the upper classes would pack small libraries in trunks and take them on their travels. Thirty or forty books would contain all the learning required of a decent individual. These libraries were not of course measured in gigabytes, but it was the same idea.

This reminds me of another, more troubling kind of contemporary short cut. In the Seventies I spent some time in a New York apartment lent to me by a film producer. The apartment contained no books, except for one shelf that held 'the masterpieces of world literature in digest form'. It was surreal: *War and Peace* in fifty pages, Balzac in a single volume. I couldn't believe my eyes. Everything was there, but incomplete and mutilated. What a massive effort, for such an absurd end.

U. E. | There's abridged and abridged. In the 1930s and '40s there was a remarkable Italian publishing experiment called 'La Scala d'Oro'. It consisted of adaptations of the gems of world literature categorised according to reader age. There was the 7–8-year-old series, the 8–9-year-old series, and so on, up to fourteen – all beautifully illustrated by the best artists of the day. In order to make them accessible to their readership, the books had each been rewritten by an accomplished children's writer. There was, of course, an element of bowdlerisation. For instance, in *Les Misérables* Javert didn't commit suicide, he merely resigned. When I read the original version at a later age, I discovered the truth about Javert. But I have to say that I had got the general idea.

J.-C. C. | The difference being that the abridged library in the producer's apartment was meant for adults. And even, I suspect, to be shown and seen, rather than read. Having said that, literature has been mutilated since time began. The first Shakespeare plays to be translated into French were done by Abbot Delille in the eighteenth century, and he gave them all positive, conventional, moral endings, like your 'Scala d'Oro' version of *Les Misérables*. For example, Hamlet didn't die. And this watered-down version was the first time – apart from some rather wonderful short passages translated by Voltaire – that the French public could read Shakespeare. This author who they had heard was bloody and barbaric was all schmaltz and chivalry.

Do you know how Voltaire translated 'To be or not to be, that is the question'? '*Arrête, il faut choisir et passer à l'instant / De la vie à la mort ou de l'être au néant.*' Not bad, actually. Some people think that Sartre borrowed his title *L'Être et le Néant* (*Being and Nothingness*) from that translation by Voltaire.

J.-P. DE T. | Jean-Claude, you describe the small libraries that the eighteenth-century educated classes travelled with as the first versions of the USB stick. Do you feel that most of our modern inventions are actually the realisation of age-old dreams?

U. E. | Dreams of flying have haunted the collective imagination since time immemorial.

J.-C. C. | I do actually think that lots of our contemporary inventions are the manifestation of very ancient dreams. For example, I recently started rereading the famous sixth book of the *Aeneid*, in which Aeneas visits the Underworld to search out the spirits that the Romans believed were the souls of both those who had already lived and those who were not yet born. In the Underworld, time does not exist. So Virgil's kingdom of souls foreshadows Einstein's spacetime. As I reread a few pages of Aeneas' journey, it occurred to me that

Virgil had created a virtual world rather like the entrails of a vast computer crowded with silent avatars. Every inhabitant has been someone, or has the potential to become someone. In the Underworld, Aeneas meets a superb young man of whom a great deal is expected, but who is in fact the Marcellus who died young. When the young man is told, 'You shall be Marcellus' ('*Tu Marcellus eris*'), we are in a virtual dimension, since the reader already knows Marcellus is dead: he has all the potentialities of a man who could have become someone legendary, perhaps even the providential saviour the world is waiting for, but in fact is only Marcellus, who died young.

It's as if Virgil had foreseen the virtual world we are currently exploring. This descent into the Underworld is a wonderful theme, which world literature has tackled in various ways. It has provided the means of conquering both space and time, and therefore penetrating the kingdom of the dead, and of ghosts, and travelling into both the past and the future, into being and nothingness. And thus achieving a kind of virtual immortality.

There's another example I've always found fascinating. In the Mahabharata, a queen by the name of Gandhari is pregnant, and finds herself unable to give birth. She needs her baby to be born before the baby carried by her sister-in-law, for the firstborn shall be king. So she asks a strapping servant woman to hit her hard on the belly with an iron bar. An iron ball pops out of her vagina and rolls onto the ground. She is about to throw it away, to get rid of it, when someone tells her to split the ball into a hundred pieces and put each piece into a jar, predicting that she will thus give birth to a hundred sons. Which is what happens. Is this not an early image of artificial insemination? Are these jars not the forerunners of our test tubes?

It's easy to think of other examples. Also in the Mahabharata, sperm is preserved, transported and reused. Or take the miracle in Calanda, where the Virgin Mary supposedly replaced a Spanish peasant's amputated leg: a precursor of the transplant. Then there are the stories of cloning, and sperm used after a man's death. And what about the wild, long-ago dreams of creatures with the head of a goat, the tail of a snake and the claws of a lion – dreams we thought had disappeared for ever, but are now resurfacing in laboratory experiments?

U. E. | It is not that the authors of the Mahabharata could see into the future. It is that the present has made real the dreams of the generations who came before us. You are quite right. The Fountain of Youth, for example, is about to become reality. We are living to a greater and greater age, and now have the possibility of ending our days still looking good.

J.-C. C. | In fifty years we will all be bionic. For instance I am looking at you, Umberto, with artificial eyes. Three years ago I had a cataract operation, and now I don't need to wear glasses for the first time in my life. And the results of that operation are guaranteed for fifty years! These days my eyes work perfectly, but one knee is giving me trouble. So I need to decide whether or not to have it replaced. There's definitely a prosthesis waiting for me somewhere. At least one.

J.-P. DE T. | We cannot predict the future. These days the present is constantly shedding its skin. The past, supposed to provide a solid and comforting point of reference, has a tendency to slip out of view. Do you think we're discussing the nature of impermanence?

J.-C. C. | The future takes no account of the past, but none of the present, either. Aircraft manufacturers are currently working on planes that will be ready in twenty years, but they are built to run on aviation fuel that may no longer be available. What really strikes me is the total disappearance of the present. We are increasingly obsessed with retro trends. The past is catching up with us so fast that soon 'retro' will simply mean last season's fashions. The future is as uncertain as ever, and the present is gradually shrinking, gradually being stolen away.

U.E. | Speaking of the past catching us up, I use my computer to listen to the best radio stations from around the world, including about forty that specialise in playing golden oldies. A few American radio stations only play music from the 1920s and '30s. The others concentrate on the 1990s, which is already considered the distant past. A recent survey proclaimed Quentin Tarantino the greatest director of all time. The people they asked must never have seen Eisenstein, Ford, Welles, Capra, etc. That's always the downfall of those kinds of surveys. In the Seventies I wrote a book called *How to Write a Thesis*, which has been translated into lots of languages. The first of my many tips was never to choose a contemporary subject. Your bibliography will either be thin or lacking in authority. Always choose a historical subject, I said. And yet most of today's theses explore contemporary issues. I receive loads of theses about my own work. It's crazy. How can you write a thesis about a guy who is still alive?

J.-C. C. | I think we have poor long-term memories precisely because of the way the recent past presses in on the present, shoving it towards a future that has taken the form of a giant question mark. Or perhaps already an exclamation mark. What has happened to the present – this wonderful moment we are experiencing, which all kinds of forces are constantly trying to take away from us? I sometimes sink back into this present moment when I'm in the countryside, and hear the church bells solemnly chiming the hour, bringing us back to ourselves, reminding us, 'Oh, look, it's only five o'clock . . .'

Like you, I travel a great deal, and lose myself in the corridors of time, in time differences; increasingly I feel the need to regain contact with this present moment, which is becoming so hard to grasp. Otherwise I would feel lost. Or perhaps even dead.

U.E. | This disappearance of the present that you are talking about is not only due to the fact that trends which used to last thirty years now last thirty days. It's also down to the obsolescence of objects that we have been discussing. I spent a few hours of my life learning to ride a bicycle, but once acquired, that knowledge lasted for ever. Now, I might spend two weeks learning some new computer programme, only for a new, seemingly indispensable version to come onto the market before I've even mastered the old one. Therefore the problem is not a loss of collective memory. It's the constantly changing nature of the present. We no longer live calmly in the present, but are continually striving to prepare ourselves for the future.

J.-C. C. | We are living in a changing, moving, renewable, ephemeral world, at exactly the same time that, paradoxically, we're living longer and longer lives. The life expectancy of our grandparents was of course shorter than our own, but they were living in an unchanging present. My uncle's grandfather was a landowner who, in January, did his accounts for the coming year. Last year's results were a solid basis on which to predict what the new year would bring. Things didn't change.

U. E. | It used to be the case that school students worked towards a final exam that punctuated a long period of learning: in Italy the *maturità*, in Germany the *Abitur*, in France the *baccalauréat*. After that your learning days were over, unless you happened to be one of the elite who went to university. The world was unchanging. You could use what you knew until the day you died, until your children died, even. People entered knowledge-retirement at the age of eighteen or twenty. These days, an employee of a company must constantly update his knowledge or risk losing his job. The rite of passage that these school-leaving exams used to represent no longer has the slightest meaning.

58

J.-C. C. | What you are saying also held true for people such as doctors. The knowledge that they had accumulated by the end of their studies would be valid for their entire career. And what you say about today's universal endless apprenticeship also goes for those who are supposedly 'retired'. Look at all the elderly people who've had to learn how to use a computer. We are doomed to be eternal students, like Trofimov in *The Cherry Orchard*. Which might actually be a good thing. In the so-called primitive cultures, which don't change in this way, it is the old who wield the power, because it is they who transmit knowledge to their children. Whereas when the world is in constant revolution, it is the children who teach their parents electronic technologies. And what will their children teach them?

Do we need to know the name of every soldier at the Battle of Waterloo?

J.-P. DE T. | You have described the contemporary challenge of finding reliable tools to preserve that which needs to be preserved. But is the function of memory to retain everything and anything?

U. E. | No, of course not. Memory – whether it's our individual memory or the collective memory that is culture – has a double function. On the one hand to preserve certain data, and on the other to allow information that does not serve us and could pointlessly encumber our brains to sink into oblivion. A culture unable to filter the heritage it receives from previous centuries brings to mind Borges' *Funes the Memorious*, in which the title character is endowed with the ability to remember everything. That is the exact opposite of culture. Culture is essentially a graveyard for books and other lost objects. Scholars are currently researching how culture is a process of tacitly abandoning certain relics of the past (thus filtering), while placing others in a kind of refrigerator, for the future. Archives and libraries are cold rooms in which we store what has come before, so that the cultural space is not cluttered, without having to relinquish those memories entirely. We can always go back to them some day in the future, should the mood take us.

A historian would probably be able to track down the name of every soldier at the Battle of Waterloo, but these names are not taught at school or even university because this level of detail is not necessary, and may even be dangerous.

Let me give you another example. We know a lot about Caesar's last wife, Calpurnia, up until the date of his assassination, the Ides of March, when she advised him not to go to the Senate on account of a bad dream she'd had. However, we know nothing at all about what happened to her after Caesar's death. She disappears from the collective memory. Why? Because there was no longer any point in knowing anything about her. And this was not, as you might suspect, because she was a woman. Clara Schumann was a woman too, but we know all about her life after Robert's death. Culture, therefore, is this process of selection. But contemporary culture is quite the opposite. The Internet drowns us in detail about every Calpurnia the world over, on a day-by-day and minute-by-minute basis, to the extent that a kid researching his homework could be forgiven for thinking that Calpurnia was just as important as Caesar.

J.-C. C. | But how do we select for the generations to come? And who will do the selection? How are we to know what will interest our descendants – what will be necessary to them, or useful, or even entertaining? How to filter when, as you say, our computers simply provide everything, without the slightest hierarchy, selection or structure? In other words, how do we build a collective memory in these conditions, knowing as we do that this memory is a matter of choices, preferences, rejections and omissions both intentional and accidental? And knowing also that the memory of our descendants won't necessarily work in the same way as ours. What will a clone's memory be like?

I am a historian by training, and I know how wary one has to be of documents purportedly giving us a precise understanding of events that happened in the past. Let me illustrate this with a personal story. My wife Nahal's father was a highly educated Iranian who, amongst other work, researched a Baghdad bookbinder from the tenth century by the name of al-Nadim. As you know, the Iranians invented bookbinding – including that binding style where a flap covers and protects the book when it's not in use.

This learned binder and calligrapher was so interested in the books he bound that he read them, and even wrote a summary of each book. Almost all the books he bound have since disappeared, leaving us with only the binder's summaries, in a catalogue he entitled *Kitab al-Fihrist*. My father-in-law, Reza Tajadod, explored in his study what exactly we can know, via the personal filtering that was the binder's precious work, of the books he held in his hands, but that we know of only through him.

U. E. | We know of some classical sculptures and paintings only through descriptions of them, called *ekprhases*. The Laocoön statue, which dates from the Hellenistic period, was found in Rome in Michelangelo's time, but identified on the basis of descriptions by Pliny the Elder.

J.-C. C. | But what does memory mean, now that we can access anything about anything, totally unfiltered – an infinite amount of information at the click of a mouse? What is the sense of the word 'memory'? One day, we'll be constantly accompanied by an electronic servant able to answer all our questions, including the ones we haven't even formed. What will be left for us to know? Once our prosthesis knows everything – absolutely everything – what will we need to learn?

U. E. | The art of synthesis.

J.-C. C. | Yes. And the act of learning itself. Because you can learn how to learn.

U. E. | Yes, learning to handle information whose authenticity we can no longer trust. This is clearly a major challenge for teachers. School kids and students use the Internet to search out the information they need for their homework, without knowing whether that information is accurate. And how could they? I encourage teachers to set their students the homework of finding ten different sources of information on a certain subject and comparing them. This requires them to exercise their critical faculties with regard to the Internet, and to learn that they can't take it all at face value.

J.-C. C. | Deciding what to read is also a matter of filtering. The papers review a dozen 'unmissable' masterpieces every week – and the same goes for every field of artistic expression.

U. E. | I have developed a theory to deal with this. Let's take non-fiction as an example. You only need to read one book in ten. With the rest, you can just flick through the bibliography and notes and you'll be able to tell whether the references are serious. If the book is important, there's no need to read it because it will be quoted and critiqued in other books, including the one you have decided to read. In any case, if you're an academic you receive such a lot of printed material before the book even comes out that you won't have time to read it once it's published.

And by the time it reaches you it is often outdated anyway. And then there are what we Italians call 'ready-baked' books – namely, books published in opportunistic response to an event, which are a complete waste of time.

J.-C. C. | When I was studying history, about fifty years ago, they would relieve the strain on our memories by providing us with the chronological events necessary for the discussion of a certain subject. We weren't made to learn dates that weren't of much interest outside the context of that particular task. But one couldn't use information from the Internet in that way without first checking its reliability. This tool – which is supposed to be comforting in its delivery of everything and anything – actually plunges us into great confusion. I suspect that the websites dedicated to Umberto Eco are full of wrong information, or at the very least inaccuracies. Will we soon need fact-checking secretaries? Will that be the start of a new profession?

U. E. | But a personal fact-checker's task would not be straightforward. You and I can certainly check facts about ourselves. But who would be the personal fact-checker of sites on French political figures like Clemenceau, for example, or Boulanger? And who would pay them? Not the French government, that's for sure, because then they'd have to employ fact-checkers for every great figure in French history!

J.-C. C. | I do think, though, that one way or another we'll have an increasing need for these checkers. It will become a widespread profession.

U. E. | But who will check on the checker? In the old days, the checkers were members of great cultural institutions, of academies and universities. When Mr So-and-So, member of Such-and-Such Institute, published his book on Clemenceau, or Plato, one assumed that the data he provided was accurate, because he would have spent his entire life checking his sources in libraries. But these days it's quite possible that Mr So-and-So also got some facts from the Internet, and so everything becomes suspect. Although, to be honest, that could have been the case before the Internet. Individual as well as collective memories are not photographs of what actually happened. They are reconstructions.

J.-C. C. | You and I both know the extent to which nationalism and its prejudices have distorted the depiction of certain historical events. Even today historians are often, almost despite themselves, governed by the explicit or implicit ideology of their country. As we speak, Chinese historians are writing all kinds of nonsense about the ancient relations between China and Tibet, and Mongolia – and this is being taught in Chinese schools. Atatürk oversaw a complete rewrite of Turkish history. He claimed that there were Turks in Turkey at the time of the Romans, centuries before they actually arrived. And so on and so forth, all over the world . . . And finding out the truth is no simple matter. We think that the Turks actually came from central Asia, and that the original inhabitants of contemporary Turkey didn't leave any written traces. But how can we be sure?

U.E. | There are similar issues with geography. It wasn't very long ago that Africa was restored to its proper dimensions, long underestimated by imperial ideologies.

J.-C. C. | I happened to go to Bulgaria recently, and in Sofia I stayed at the Arena di Serdica hotel, which I didn't know. As I arrived I noticed that the hotel had been built on ruins, which could still be seen through a big sheet of glass. I asked the hotel staff about it. They explained that there had been a Roman coliseum on the very same spot. Astonishing! I never knew the Romans had built a coliseum in Sofia – and then the staff told me that it was only ten metres smaller in diameter than the one in Rome. Vast, then. And archaeologists had discovered sculptures on the external walls that functioned like posters, describing the shows due to take place inside. They featured dancers, gladiators of course, and something I hadn't come across before – a battle between a crocodile and a lion.

My conception of Bulgaria, already turned upside down a few years before by the discovery of Thracian treasures (meaning that this part of the world goes way back, further even than Greece) was rocked to its very foundations. And why had the Romans built this enormous circus in Sofia? Because they were very fond, apparently, of the Sofia hot springs. I remembered then that Sofia isn't far from where poor old Ovid was sent into exile. And now Bulgaria, which I had always believed to have thoroughly Slavic roots, was suddenly a Roman colony!

The past never stops surprising us – more than the present, more perhaps even than the future. Let me conclude my story of a suddenly Roman Bulgaria with this aphorism from the Bavarian comic Karl Valentin: 'In the past, even the future was better.' We also owe to Valentin this very sensible remark: 'Everything has been said already, but not yet by everyone.'

We have now reached a stage in our history when we can delegate the task of remembering both the good and the bad things to intelligent – or so we think –

machines. The philosopher Michel Serres touched on this in an interview that appeared in the education supplement of *Le Monde*. He said that if we no longer need to be able to remember, then 'intelligence is all we have left'.

U. E. | I agree that there doesn't seem to be much point in learning times tables in an era when machines can count better than anyone. But there is the issue of keeping in shape. I can clearly travel much faster by car than on foot. And yet if I don't want to become a couch potato, I need to walk or run a little every day. I expect you already know that wonderful science-fiction story set in the twenty-second century, when computers do all our thinking for us. The Pentagon discovers someone who still knows his times tables by heart. They conclude he is some kind of genius, and particularly valuable in wartime, in case the world suffers a global power cut.

There's another problem. In certain cases, the fact of knowing certain things by heart improves your intellect. I quite agree that being cultured is not a matter of knowing the exact date of Napoleon's death. But there's no doubt that the sum total of what one can retain in one's own brain, even the date of Napoleon's death – 5th May 1821 – does give one a certain intellectual freedom.

This is not a new debate. The invention of printing created the possibility of storing all the cultural information one does not wish to be burdened with 'in the fridge' – that is to say, in books – whilst knowing that the information could be found whenever it was needed. Aspects of memory can be delegated to books, and to machines, but we still have to know how to use these tools to their maximum effect. So we still need to keep our own minds and memories in good shape.

J.-C. C. | But no one could argue with the fact that in order to use these sophisticated tools – which, as we have seen, tend to become obsolete – we are constantly having to learn and remember new languages and functions. So our memory is in great demand. Perhaps more so than ever.

U. E. | And you can't rely on these tools to keep things safe. Anyone who hasn't been able to keep up to date with their data storage since the first computers in 1983, moving from floppy disks to mini disks to compact discs to memory sticks, will have lost some or all of their archive several times over. None of our contemporary computers can read the first floppy disks; they already belong to the prehistory of information technology. I searched desperately for an early version of my novel *Foucault's Pendulum,* which I must have copied onto a disk in 1984 or '85, but I couldn't find it anywhere. If I had written the novel on a typewriter, I would still have it.

J.-C. C. | There is perhaps something that doesn't die, and that's our memory of what we have been through at certain times in our lives. Our precious, and sometimes deceptive, memories of feelings and emotions. Our emotional memory. Who would want to delegate that, and why?

U. E. | But our biological memory function has to be exercised on a daily basis. If our memory were like that of a floppy disk, we'd have Alzheimer's at the age of fifty. One way to stave off Alzheimer's, or senile dementia of any kind, is to keep learning – for example, a new poem by heart every morning. Doing all kinds of intellectual exercises. Word games and anagrams, even. Our generation was still forced to learn poems by heart at school, but that's happening less and less. What we were doing with this rote-learning was simply exercising our memories, and therefore our intelligence. We are no longer forced to do it, so now we must impose this daily challenge on ourselves, or risk early senility.

J.-C. C. | May I qualify what you have said in two ways? It's true that memory – and probably the imagination – is in some sense a muscle that can be trained. Not that we want to become Borges' Funes, whom you were mentioning just now: a man who remembers everything, and has lost the sweet luxury of forgetting. However, no one has learned more texts by heart than theatre actors. And yet, despite a lifetime of training, there are many cases of Alzheimer's among them, which I have always found rather curious. I am struck, as you probably are too, by the coincidence between the development of seemingly infinite artificial memories stored in our computers and the increasing prevalence of Alzheimer's disease. It's as if machines are supplanting humans, making our own memories seem pathetic and useless. We no longer need to be our full selves. It's extraordinary – and terrifying too, don't you think?

U. E. | It is definitely important to distinguish between function and the physical thing itself. For example, walking exercises my leg's function and keeps it in good shape, but if I broke my leg I would no longer be able to walk. One could say the same thing about the brain. Clearly, if our grey matter is afflicted by some kind of physical degeneration, the fact of having learned ten verses of Racine by heart every day will not be enough.

75

A friend of mine called Giorgio Prodi (Romano's brother) was a famous cancer specialist, who died of cancer despite his brain knowing everything there was to know about the subject. He said to me: 'If in the future we all live to be a hundred, most of us will die of cancer.' The longer our life expectancies, the more likely that our bodies will start going wrong. What I'm trying to say is that this prevalence of Alzheimer's may just be a consequence of people living longer.

J.-C. C. | Objection, Your Honour. I recently read an article in a medical journal saying that Alzheimer's is occurring younger and younger. Some people are developing it at the age of forty-five.

U. E. | OK. In that case I'll stop learning poems by heart, and start drinking two bottles of whisky a day. Thanks for giving me hope.

J.-C. C. | My memory must be working OK, because I've just remembered the perfect quote: 'I remember a man who had a remarkable memory. But I can't remember what he knew.' All I remember, therefore, is forgetting. Having said that, it seems to me that this stage of our conversation brings us to the distinction in the French language between learning (*savoir*) and knowledge (*connaissance*). Learning is what we are burdened with, and which may not always be useful to us. Knowledge is the transformation of that learning into a life experience. So perhaps we can delegate this constantly renewed learning to machines, and focus our energies on knowledge. This is how we must understand Michel Serres. Our intelligence is all that is left to us, and that's a relief. We should add that all this soul-searching and debate about memory will seem utterly pompous and absurd, should a major ecological crisis destroy humanity, wiping us out in a single event, or simply because we are no longer able to survive. I'm reminded of the final sentence in Lévi-Strauss' *Mythologiques:* 'and were as nothing'. 'Nothing' is the last word. Our last word.

The revenge of the filtered-out

J.-P. DE T. | Perhaps we should return to the situation created by the unverifiable collective memory that is the Internet. How should we handle this material and these contradictions, in all their diversity and abundance?

J.-C. C. | What the Internet provides is gross information, with almost no sense of order or hierarchy, and with the sources unchecked. So each of us needs not only to check facts, but also to create meaning, by which I mean to organise and position our learning within an argument. But according to what criteria? As we have said, our history books were often written with a national or ideological bias, and were also influenced by all kinds of other transient interests. There is no such thing as a pure or objective history of the French Revolution. According to French historians working in the nineteenth century, Danton was the great man: many streets were named after him and statues built in his honour. But then he was disgraced by a charge of corruption, and Robespierre the Incorruptible returned to favour, bolstered by Marxist historians such as Albert Matthiez. A few streets were named after Robespierre in the communist suburbs of Paris, and even a metro station at Montreuil-sous-Bois. Who, or what, will be in favour next? We don't know. Thus we need an angle, or at least some reference points, to help us tackle this stormy sea of information.

U. E. | I see another threat. Culture filters things, telling us what we should retain and what we must forget. In this way it gives us some common ground, with regard to mistakes as well as truths. The Galilean revolution can only be understood from the starting point of Ptolemy's work. We have to enter the Ptolemaic mindset, in order to reach the Galilean phase and understand the nature of Ptolemy's mistake. Discussions between people can only take place on the basis of a shared encyclopaedia. I could prove to you that Napoleon never existed – but only because all three of us have learned that he did. That is what ensures that dialogue can continue. It is this intercourse that allows for dialogue, creativity and freedom. As you have just said, the Internet gives us everything and forces us to filter it not by the workings of culture, but with our own brains. This risks creating six billion separate encyclopaedias, which would prevent any common understanding whatsoever.

We're somewhat in the realm of science fiction here, because there will always be factors encouraging people to subscribe to similar beliefs. There will always be the acknowledged authority of what we call the international scientific community, which is trusted because we see that it is able to critique and publicly correct itself on a daily basis. It is because of our trust in the scientific community that we can take it on blind faith that the square root of 2 is 1.41421356237309504880168872420969807856967187537694 807317667973799073 (I don't know that off by heart, I just looked it up on my palmtop). I mean, what other kind of guarantee does a layperson have that this is true? One might say that scientific truths will remain more or less universally accepted because if we didn't share the same mathematical ideas, it would become impossible to build a house.

Having said that, you don't have to surf the Internet for long to discover groups of people questioning ideas we might have thought were universally accepted – asserting, for instance, that the Earth is hollow and we are living on its inner surface, or that the world really was created in six days. So there's the danger of encountering lots of contradictory information. We expected globalisation to make everyone start thinking alike. What has actually happened is precisely the opposite: globalisation has led to the parcelling up of common experience into different camps.

J.-C. C. | This profusion of ideas through which each of us is forced to carve his own path reminds me of the Hindu pantheon, with its 36,000 major deities and infinite number of secondary deities. Despite this dispersal of the divine, there are some important gods worshipped by all Hindus. Why? In India, there is a perspective known as the 'perspective of the tortoise'. You put a tortoise on the floor with its four toes emerging from under its shell. These toes represent the four cardinal directions. You stand on the tortoise, which is one of the manifestations of Vishnu, and select from among the 36,000 divinities you see around you those that speak to you most strongly. And then you set off on your journey.

To me this is very like the personal journey that we can take through the Internet. Every Hindu has his personal deities. And yet Hindus share a community of belief. But this brings us back to filtering. Our education is the result of filtering that took place before our time. As you have reminded us, that is the nature of culture. But we can of course challenge these filters, as we frequently do. Here's an example – for me, the greatest French poets apart from Rimbaud and Baudelaire are largely unknown. They are the baroque poets of the early seventeenth century, to whom Boileau and the classicists dealt a sudden death. Their names are Jean de la Ceppède, Jean-Baptiste Chassignet, Claude Hopil and Pierre de Marbeuf. I know some of their poems by heart, but they can only be found in first editions, which is to say published at the time, and therefore rare and expensive. They have almost never been republished. I repeat that they are among the best French poets, superior by far to Lamartine or Alfred de Musset, who are sold to us as the most distinguished of our poets. Musset published fourteen volumes of poetry; I was delighted to discover that Alfred Jarry had called him fourteen times crap.

Our past, therefore, is not set in stone. Nothing is more alive than the past. Allow me to go a little further. When I adapted Edmond Rostand's *Cyrano de Bergerac* for the cinema, Jean-Paul Rappeneau and I wanted to focus on the character of Roxane, rather neglected in the play. I used to enjoy describing *Cyrano* to people as the story of a woman. 'What do you mean the story of a woman?' they'd say. Yes, it's the story of a woman who has found the perfect man – handsome, intelligent and generous – but with one drawback: he is in fact two men.

Roxane had a great appreciation for these poets, the poets of her time. I helped the actress Anne Brochet get to know her character (an intelligent, sensitive, provincial woman who has come to Paris), by lending her first editions of these forgotten poets. Anne not only enjoyed them, she read their work with me at the Avignon Festival. It is thus possible to resuscitate the unjustly forgotten dead, if only for a moment.

And I am speaking of the dead, quite literally. We

must remember that some of these poets were burned in the place de Grève – and this was in the seventeenth century – on account of being libertines, rebels, often homosexual and always provocative. This happened to Jacques Chausson. We still have one of Claude Petit's sonnets, written about the death of his friend, who was convicted of sodomy and debauchery and burned at the stake in 1661. The executioners used to clothe the prisoner in a sulphur-soaked shirt, so that the fire would set him alight very fast and choke him to death. 'Friends, they have burned poor Chausson,' is the first line of Petit's sonnet. He describes the dreadful execution, finishing with an allusion to the blazing sulphur shirt: 'He died rather like he lived / The scoundrel, showing his arse to the world.'

Claude Petit was burned to death himself, a year later. Not many people know that. These were the years of Corneille and Molière, we were building Versailles, it was our 'Great Century'. This, then, is another type of filtering: burning people to death. Happily, at the end of the nineteenth century a bibliophile by the name of Frédéric Lachèvre became fascinated by these poets and republished them in small print runs for the love of it. Thanks to him, we can still read their work.

U. E. | You're talking of forgotten French baroque poets. For the first half of the twentieth century the majority of

Italian baroque poetry was totally neglected in Italian school curriculums, because it was considered such a decadent time. I am of the generation who discovered baroque at university, rather than school, and then thanks to radical lecturers; this discovery actually inspired my novel *The Island of the Day Before*. But our generation has also contributed to changing conceptions of the Middle Ages, a revision that started in the second half of the nineteenth century. At one point I was working on medieval aesthetics. A handful of talented scholars had done some superb work on the subject, but the intellectual classes were still dismissive and one had to be very determined. But the French lack of awareness of those baroqe poets is perhaps also due to the fact that France did not have a true baroque period in architecture. By the seventeenth century French architecture was already classical, whereas in Italy the architects Bernini and Borromini were creating work that is the physical equivalent of the poetry you were talking about. The French never experienced that fever of baroque architecture. The church of Saint-Sulpice is not baroque. Not that I would ever be so naughty as to agree with Huysmans that it's the model for all French railway stations.

J.-C. C. | Which didn't stop him from setting part of his novel *The Damned* there.

U. E. | The Loire chateaux such as the chateau de Chambord may actually, despite having been designed during the Renaissance, be the only true examples of French baroque.

J.-C. C. | In Germany, baroque is the equivalent of classical architecture.

U. E. | That's why they consider Andreas Gryphius a great poet. This makes me think of something else that could explain why baroque had more impact in some places than others. In Italy, baroque arose in the midst of a period of political decadence, whereas at the same time in France the state was becoming considerably stronger. A powerful king cannot allow his architects to indulge their dreams. Baroque is both libertarian and anarchic.

J.-C. C. | Rebellious, almost. At the time, France was heavily influenced by Boileau's dreadful lines: 'Then came Malherbe, the greatest France had known / His verse good and true, in the proper even tone'. Boileau, the anti-poet of them all. Speaking of that Taliban-like time, we should also mention Baltasar Gracian, another long-underrated and recently rediscovered figure, and author notably of *The Art of Worldly Wisdom*.

U. E. | He had an important contemporary, too: while Gracian was working on his book in Spain, Torquato Accetto was writing *Of Honest Dissembling* in Italy. Gracian and Accetto agree on many points. But while Gracian recommends adopting a false court persona in the interests of courtly success, Accetto's motive in suggesting behaviour that allows a person to hide his real self is primarily self-protection. These are of course subtle differences between the authors of two tracts on simulation – one is foregrounding appearances, the other disappearances.

J.-C. C. | There is clearly one Italian author dealing with such subjects who has never required rescuing: Machiavelli. But tell me, do you think any great scientists have been unjustly forgotten in this way?

U. E. | Science is murderous, but it works differently. It murders the previous idea, as soon as it is invalidated by a more recent discovery. For instance, scientists used to think that waves were transmitted through the ether. But as soon as they proved that ether didn't exist, the theory became unmentionable, and was relegated to scientific history. Unfortunately, American analytical philosophy has adopted this stance too, in its desperation to be considered a science. Just a few decades ago a sign in the philosophy department at Princeton used to read 'Historians of philosophy not admitted'. But actually the human sciences must never forget their history. An analytical philosopher once asked me why he should give a damn what the Stoics had said about such-and-such an issue. Either it was rubbish, and therefore of no interest, or it was a valid idea, and one of them would probably come up with it sooner or later.

I replied that the Stoics had perhaps raised some interesting questions that had since been abandoned and needed to be resurrected with the greatest of urgency. If Stoic thinking was correct, then I couldn't see why we should wait for some American genius to rediscover an idea that the most ill-educated European was already aware of. On the other hand, if the development of such-and-such an idea formulated in ancient times had led to a dead end, it would be as well to know that now, rather than embarking again on a road that led nowhere.

J.-C. C. | I would like to add something about the eighteenth century. During the 120 or 130 years between Racine's *Phèdre* and the Romantics, not a single poem was written in France. Versifiers did of course churn out and publish thousands, if not millions, of lines of verse, but you won't find a French person today who can quote a single one. I could mention Jean-Pierre Claris de Florian, a mediocre fable-writer, the Abbot

Delille or Jean-Baptiste Rousseau, but who has read them, and more importantly who could read them today? Who can still read Voltaire's tragedies? They were highly regarded at the time, their author was the darling of the Comédie-Française, but these days they bore us to death. The thing is that these so-called 'poets' merely applied the previous century's rules as decreed by Boileau. Never have so many verses been written, and so few poems. Not a single one in more than a century. When you do nothing but apply a set of rules, the elements of surprise, brilliance and inspiration all evaporate. I sometimes try to impress this on young film-makers. 'You can carry on making films, that's relatively easy – but it's not cinema.'

U. E. | In this particular case, the filtering process has merit. We are better off forgetting these 'poets' you've been talking about.

J.-C. C. | Yes, it's a case of ruthless and appropriate filtering. They've all been despatched to the depths of oblivion. It seems to me that the era's talent, innovation and daring belonged more to the philosophers, to prose writers such as Laclos, Lesage and Diderot, and to two playwrights: Marivaux and Beaumarchais. Until the nineteenth century, our great era of the novel.

U.E. | The great era of the English novel, on the other hand, was the eighteenth century, with Samuel Richardson, Daniel Defoe . . . The three great homes of the novel are definitely France, England and Russia.

J.-C. C. | But it's amazing how artistic inspiration can suddenly vanish. If you were describing the history of French poetry from, say, François Villon to the Surrealists, you would mention the schools that successively dominated the world of poetry: the Pléiade group, the classical poets, the Romantics, the Symbolists, the Surrealists, etc. But you wouldn't be able to find any poetic legacy, or new inspiration, in the entire period between 1676, when *Phèdre* was written, and the work of an author such as André Chénier.

U.E. | A poetic silence that corresponds to one of the most glorious periods in French history.

J.-C. C. | In which French was the diplomatic language throughout Europe. But I've looked, I promise! Even in popular verse; everywhere. There was nothing worth saving.

U.E. | Literary and pictorial movements are created through imitation and influence. Let's say, for example, that a certain author writes a rather good and successful historical novel: he will immediately be plagiarised. The discovery that romantic novels are good money-spinners encourages others to try their hand. For example, the so-called 'novel of manners' was born in England under very particular economic circumstances. Authors wrote novels for the wives of sailors and merchants, who knew how to read and had the time to do so because their husbands were away working. But they also wrote them for their lady's maids, who like their mistresses had access to candles, and so could read at night-time. The novel of manners was born out of a trading economy, and aimed mainly at women. And as soon as people realised that Mr Richardson was making money by telling the story of a lady's maid, there were plenty of pretenders to his throne.

J.-C. C. | Creative trends often stem from small groups of people who know each other and share the same tastes at the same time. Friends, almost. All the Surrealists I have ever had the good fortune to meet have told me that they felt drawn to Paris shortly after the end of the First World War. Man Ray came from America, Max Ernst from Germany, Buñuel and Dalí from Spain, Benjamin Péret from Toulouse – all of them came to Paris to meet people like themselves, with whom they could create new images and languages.

The same thing happened with the Beat generation, the French New Wave, the Italian film-makers who gathered in Rome, etc. Even the Iranian poets of the twelfth and thirteenth centuries, who came out of nowhere. I'd like to name these wonderful poets – Attar, Rumi, Saadi, Hafiz, Omar Khayyám. Anyway, these individuals all knew each other and all acknowledged what you've just been talking about – the importance of the frontrunner. Then suddenly conditions change, the inspiration dries up, the groups sometimes destroy themselves and always go their separate ways, and the adventure comes to an end. In the case of Iran, the horrific Mongol invasions also played their part.

U. E. | There's a wonderful book by Allan Chapman that describes a remarkable blossoming of physics in the seventeenth century around Oxford's Royal Society, on account of the series of first-rate scholars who influenced each other as they worked and studied there. Thirty years later it was all over. The same thing happened with mathematicians in Cambridge at the beginning of the twentieth century.

J.-C. C. | So it's hard to believe in the myth of the isolated genius. The Pléiade poets – Ronsard, du Bellay, Marot – were all friends. The same goes for the French classicists. Molière, Racine, Corneille and Boileau all knew each other, to the extent that people could suggest – absurdly – that Corneille actually wrote Molière's plays. The great Russian novelists wrote to each other, and even to their counterparts in France: Turgenev and Flaubert, for example, were correspondents. If an author wishes to avoid being filtered out, he is better off joining forces and becoming part of a group than going solo.

U. E. | The mystery around Shakespeare stems from the fact that it's hard to understand how a simple actor could have given birth to such a superb body of work. But in fact, Shakespeare was not isolated. He was surrounded by educated people, among them the other Elizabethan poets.

J.-C. C. | Now for a question I'm not sure it's possible to answer. Why do certain periods appear to select one artistic medium to the exclusion of all others? Painting and architecture in Italy during the Renaissance; poetry in sixteenth-century England; theatre followed by philosophy in seventeenth-century France; the novel in Russia and France the following century, etc. I have always wondered, for example, what Buñuel would have done with his life if film had not yet been invented. I'm also thinking of François Truffaut's categorical statement: 'There is no English cinema, and no French theatre.' As if theatre were English, and cinema French. Which is obviously a little hasty.

U. E. | You're right to say that it's impossible to solve a mystery like that. One would have to take such a huge number of factors into account. A bit like trying to forecast the position of a tennis ball in the ocean at any particular moment. Why the absence of great painters in Shakespeare's England, whereas Giotto was painting in Dante's Italy, and Raphael in Ariosto's? How did the École Française come into being? One could always say that King Francis I brought Leonardo da Vinci to France, and that da Vinci sowed the seeds of what would become the École Française. But what exactly would that explain?

J.-C. C. | Allow me to linger for a nostalgic moment on the birth of that wonderful era of Italian film-making. Why did this phenomenon appear in Italy, and why just at the end of the Second World War? Centuries of painting colliding with an unusual determination on the part of young film-makers to portray the life of a nation? Easy to say. We can analyse the circumstances as much as we like, but the real reasons will never be known. Especially if we ask ourselves: and why did it disappear so suddenly?

I have often thought of Rome's film studios Cinecittà as rather like a large painting studio in which Titian, Veronese, Tintoretto and their apprentices were all working at the same time. I'm sure you know that when the Pope called Titian to Rome, his retinue was said to be more than four miles long. It was like a massive film studio moving location. But is this enough to explain the birth of neo-realism and Italian comedy? And the work of Visconti, Antonioni and Fellini?

J.-P. DE T. | Is it possible to imagine a culture that has never given birth to any form of art?

U. E. | It's very hard to say. There are parts of the world where that was thought to be the case. But all it took was a visit and a little research to discover artistic traditions that we simply hadn't recognised as such.

J.-C. C. | It's also important to realise that in the ancient traditional cultures, there was no cult of the great artist. Superb artists existed, but they didn't sign their work. And they didn't think of themselves, nor were they thought of, as artists.

U. E. | Nor do some cultures have the notion of innovation that is the hallmark of the Western world: what 'artists' strive to do is create faithful repetitions of the same decorative patterns, and to pass down this age-old learning to their students. Any variations that there may be in their art are imperceptible to us. When I visited Australia I was very struck by the lives of the Aborigines. Not the ones who have now been almost totally destroyed by alcohol and our supposed civilisation, but the Aborigines who lived on the land before the Westerners arrived. What did they do in those days? Their nomadic journeys through the massive Australian desert took them round and round in circles. In the evenings they would catch and eat a lizard or a snake, and in the mornings set off again. If they had proceeded in a straight line for a little while, instead of travelling in circles, they would have come to the sea where all manner of riches awaited them. Their painting – both contemporary and ancient – is an extremely beautiful, abstract-looking art made up entirely of circles. During my stay we visited an Aboriginal reservation, which included a Christian church complete with priest. The priest showed us a huge mosaic at the far end of the building consisting, of course, of circles. The priest told us that according to the Aborigines these circles represented (and he couldn't explain how) the Passion of Christ. However, my son, who was a teenager at the time and rather lacking in religious education, noticed that there were fourteen circles; these must have been the fourteen Stations of the Cross.

They had thus portrayed the Way of the Cross as a sort of continuous circular movement punctuated by fourteen stations. They had been unable to separate themselves from the symbols and imagination of their culture – and yet within this culture of repetition there was some innovation. But we mustn't get carried away. Let's come back to baroque. We have explained the lack of baroque in France by saying that the central power of the monarchy was very strong, and that this central power was only willing to condone a rather classical architecture. Which probably also explains why the period you have been talking about – the late seventeenth and the eighteenth centuries – lacked poetic inspiration. The great French nation of the time demanded a kind of discipline antithetical to artistic life.

J.-C. C. | One could almost say that France's most glorious period was the one in which she deprived herself of poetry. She was almost without feeling, or voice. At the same time, Germany was experiencing the uprising of *Sturm und Drang*. I sometimes wonder whether our contemporary rulers – men like Berlusconi and Sarkozy, who love to boast that they don't read – are not rather nostalgic for a time when impertinent voices could be silenced and power was straightforward. Our president seems at times to have a constitutional dislike for that first great French psychological novel, *The Princess of Cleves*; as a busy man, he can't see the point of students reading it and seems to need to say so repeatedly. Imagine all the authors we could condemn to the long silence of the pointless, and bury alongside Madame de La Fayette. Speaking of which, you Italians never had a Sun King.

U. E. | No, but we had sun princes, who ran the cities and encouraged exceptional creativity right up to the seventeenth century. We have been in slow decline ever since. In fact our equivalent of your Sun King was the Pope, and so it's no coincidence that it was under the reign of the great pontiffs that our architecture and painting were particularly fecund, although not literature. The great period of Italian literature was the one in which poets worked for the rulers of small cities such as Florence and Ferrara, rather than for Rome.

J.-C. C. | We are still discussing the filtering process – but how to analyse its workings when we don't have the luxury of distance? Let's imagine I was asked to describe Louis Aragon and his place in French literary history. What could I say? Aragon and Paul Éluard were shaped by Surrealism, but later wrote dreadful pro-communist

hype such as 'The universe of Stalin is forever reborn
. . .' Éluard will certainly be remembered as a poet,
and Aragon perhaps as a novelist. Yet what I actually
remember of Aragon are his songs, put to music by
Brassens and others. I am still very fond of those songs;
they were such an important part of my youth. But
I'm aware that they represent a single moment in the
whole of cultural history. What will remain for future
generations?

Another example from the world of film. When I
was a student, fifty years ago, cinema was around fifty
years old. We had wonderful teachers, whom we
learned to admire and whose works we analysed
minutely. One of those teachers was René Clair.
Buñuel used to say about the 1930s that there were
three directors who could do anything: Chaplin, Walt
Disney and René Clair. No one at film school today
has heard of René Clair. People barely remember his
name. The same goes for Buñuel's beloved 1930s
Germans: Georg Wilhelm Pabst, Fritz Lang and
Murnau. Who knows them, who quotes from them,
who uses them in examples? Fritz Lang will definitely
survive – for film lovers at least – because of *M*. But
not the others. We can therefore see that the filtering
takes place invisibly and imperceptibly, within the
film schools themselves, and that it's the students
who decide. Sometimes one of the 'filtered-out'

suddenly reappears, when a film of his is shown some-where and has a big impact. Or perhaps someone has written a book about him. But this happens very rarely. So you could say that just as cinema is starting to become part of history, it is also being forgotten.

U. E. | The same thing goes for the three great Italian poets of the turn of the century: d'Annunzio, Carducci and Pascoli. D'Annunzio was our most celebrated national poet up until fascism. After the war, they realised that Pascoli's work had foreshadowed twentieth-century poetry. At that point Carducci was seen as a rhetorician and rather dismissed. But there is now a movement to resurrect him and show that he was really rather good.

The three stars of the following generation were Giuseppe Ungaretti, Eugenio Montale and Umberto Saba. There was much discussion as to which of them should be awarded the Nobel Prize, but in 1959 it went to Salvatore Quasimodo. Montale was definitely the best twentieth-century Italian poet (and I think one of the finest in the world), and he only received his Nobel in 1975.

J.-C. C. | For twenty-five or thirty years, my generation thought Italian cinema was the best in the world. Every month we would eagerly anticipate the release of two or three Italian films, and never dream of missing them. They were part of our lives, not just our education. But then, one sad day, the films went downhill and the scene suddenly died. We were told that it was mostly the fault of Italian television, which co-produced the films. But I'm sure that the scene also suffered from the mysterious phenomenon of burnout that we've been discussing. Suddenly the vitality is gone, the directors and actors are getting old, the work becomes repetitive and an essential part of the magic is lost. That school of Italian film-making no longer exists, but it was definitely one of the greats.

And what from those thirty years of laughter and excitement has stood the test of time? I still find Fellini enchanting. It seems that Antonioni still has a great reputation. Have you seen his final short, *Michelangelo Eye-to-Eye*? It's one of the most beautiful films in the world. Antonioni shot it in 2000. Not a single word is spoken for the whole fifteen minutes. Antonioni directed himself, which he'd never done before. We see him enter Rome's Church of St-Peter-in-Chains, alone. He slowly approaches the tomb of Pope Julius II. The whole film is a wordless dialogue, an exchange of gazes between Antonioni and Michelangelo's *Moses*. Everything we have been talking about, our era's obsession with appearances and words, its senseless agitation, is put into question by the fact of this silence, by the film-maker's gaze. He has come to say goodbye. He won't be coming back, and he knows it. The departing man has come to pay a final visit to the impenetrable masterpiece that will remain. As if trying one last time to understand. As if trying to solve a mystery that is beyond words. Antonioni's final glance at Moses is moving in the extreme.

U. E. | It seems to me that recently Antonioni has been rather forgotten. Fellini, on the other hand, has become more and more famous since he died.

J.-C. C. | Antonioni is definitely my favourite, even if he still doesn't have quite the reputation he deserves.

U. E. | Fellini lived in a time of intense political commitment, and was seen as a dreamer, as someone not interested in social issues. Watching his films again after his death allows us to reassess his work. I recently saw *La Dolce Vita* on TV. It's an absolute masterpiece.

J.-C. C. | I sometimes worry that the film-makers who were almost gods to us when I was young may one day be forgotten. As a teenager, the director Milos Forman was inspired to make films by watching Italian neo-realist cinema, especially the films of Vittorio De Sica.

For him there was Italian film on the one hand, and Chaplin on the other.

U. E. | We're back at our hypothesis. When the state is too powerful, poetry stagnates. When the state is in crisis, as has been the case in Italy since just after the war, then art is free to say what it has to say. The great era of neo-realism took place when Italy was in pieces. The so-called 'Italian miracle' (the industrial and commercial boom of the 1950s) had not yet begun. *Rome, Open City* was made in 1945, *Paisà* in 1947, and *Bicycle Thieves* in 1948. Similarly, Venice was still a major commercial power in the eighteenth century, but starting to decline. And it produced Tiepolo, Canaletto, Guardi and Goldini. So as power fades, some art forms are given a boost, and some not.

J.-C. C. | Not a single book published in France between 1800 and 1814 – the zenith of Napoleon's power – is still read today. The painting was pompous, not to say pretentious. Jean-Louis David had been a wonderful painter, but with the *Coronation of Napoleon* his work became flat and lifeless. He ended up rather a sad case, painting mawkish classical subjects in Belgium. Neither was there any music. Or theatre. Corneille's work was performed over and over again. Madame de Staël was forced to leave the country. Chateaubriand was hated by the authorities. His masterpiece *Mémoires d'outre-tombe* was started in secret and only part-published during his lifetime, and that many years later. The novels that made him famous are, I'm afraid, quite unreadable today. Now that's a strange instance of filtering: we are bored stiff by what he wrote for a large readership, and delighted by what we wrote for himself, in private.

U. E. | The same goes for Petrarch. He devoted his life to his Latin epic *Africa*, convinced that it would become the new *Aeneid* and make him famous. He only wrote the sonnets that have made him so famous when he had nothing better to do.

J.-C. C. | This notion of filtering out naturally makes me think of wine that is filtered before drinking. You can now buy wine that is sold 'unfiltered'. It retains the impurities that sometimes lend a wine its particular flavour, and that are removed during the filtering process. Perhaps the literature we tasted at school had been too heavily filtered, and therefore lacked the spice of impurity.

Every book published today is
a post-incunabulum

J.-P. DET. | This conversation is made all the more interesting by you both being not only authors, but book collectors, who have spent time and money tracking down rare, expensive books. Would you be prepared to divulge your collecting criteria?

J.-C. C. | First let me tell you a story I heard from Peter Brook. The great Edward Gordon Craig – the Stanislavsky of British theatre – found himself at rather a loose end in occupied Paris during the Second World War. He had a small apartment and a bit of money, and obviously couldn't return to England, so he kept himself busy by browsing the second-hand bookstalls on the banks of the Seine. He bought two books there, rather at random. The first was an index of Paris streets from the years when the Directory ruled France, listing the people who lived at each number. The second was an upholsterer and furniture seller's notebook from the same period, in which the man had jotted down his appointments.

Craig spent two years comparing the index and the appointment book, so as to establish the exact journeys made by the upholsterer. The information the tradesman had inadvertently supplied allowed Craig to piece together various romances and even adulterous affairs that took place under the Directory. Peter Brook, who knew Craig well and so appreciated the detailed nature of his research, told me that the stories he uncovered were absolutely fascinating.

Like Craig, I love owning books that have belonged to others before me. As I've already said, I have a particular taste for what you might call popular, or even burlesque and grotesque, French literature from the early seventeenth century, which has been generally underappreciated. I once came across a book that had been morocco-bound at the time of the Directory, so almost two centuries after it was originally printed. This would have been a great honour for such a cheap book – and means there must have been someone living under the Directory who shared my tastes, at a time when no one was interested in literature like that.

I also have a book by the Surrealist writer René Crevel, inscribed to Jacques Rigaut. Both men committed suicide. To me that book, and that book alone, is a kind of ghostly, bloody link between two men somehow brought closer by their deaths.

U. E. | I own some books whose value comes not so much from their content or the rarity of the edition as from the traces left on them by an unknown reader, who has underlined the text, sometimes in different colours, or written notes in the margin . . . For example, I've got an old Paracelsus so heavily annotated that the print is almost embroidered upon: every page looks like a piece of lace. I always tell myself it isn't right to annotate old or precious books – but then imagine an ancient book with handwritten notes by James Joyce . . . now that would be something.

J.-C. C. | Some people think there are two kinds of books. The book the author writes, and the one the reader owns. For me the owner is of interest, too. What they call 'provenance' – this book 'belonged to so-and-so'. For instance, it would be very wonderful to own a book that was once in Cardinal Mazarin's personal library. Or a book bound by one of the great nineteenth-century Paris bookbinders, who refused to bind just any old book. Even today, the fact that a book was bound by Marius-Michel or Trautz-Bauzonnet is proof that, to them, it was a book of some worth. A bit like that Iranian bookbinder I was telling you about, who took the trouble to read and summarise every book. What's more, if you wanted your book bound by Trautz-Bauzonnet, you might have had to wait five years.

U. E. | I own an incunabulum of the influential and deadly witch-hunting manual, the *Malleus Maleficarum*. It was bound by a certain 'Horned Moses', which is to say a

Jew, who worked for the Cistercian libraries only, and who did in fact sign each binding (in itself rather a rare practice by the end of the fifteenth century) with an image of a Moses with horns. What a story that is!

J.-C. C. | The story of a book can bring alive the story of an entire civilisation, as you showed so brilliantly with *The Name of the Rose*. In the religions of the Book, the book has served not only as a container or receptacle but also as a 'wide-angle lens' from which to view everything and tell everything, and perhaps decide it as well. It has been the point of arrival and of departure – giving us our image of the world, and of the end of the world too. But let me return to Iran for a moment, to the land of Mani, a Christian heretic who founded Manichaeism, and whom the Mazdeans adopted as one of their own. Mani's major criticism of Jesus was that he had not written down his teachings.

U. E. | He did once, in the sand.

J.-C. C. | If only Jesus had written, said Mani, instead of leaving it to others, how unquestionable his words would have been! But so be it. He preferred to speak. The book wasn't yet what it is to us, and Jesus wasn't Virgil. But while we're speaking of precursors to the book, I would like to return for a moment to the Roman volumina or scrolls, and the issue of the adaptation required by ever-new tools and techniques. There's a paradox here. When we scroll through a document on our screens, aren't we in some way repeating what the readers of the volumina did all those years ago, when they unwound a text rolled around a wooden pole, as newspapers still are in certain old cafés in Vienna?

U. E. | Except that the scrolling was not vertical, as on our computers, but horizontal. And then there were the synoptic Gospels, which were written on two juxtaposed columns read from left to right as the scroll unwound. Given that these scrolls were heavy, people probably had to read them on a table.

J.-C. C. | Or else have two slaves unwind them.

U. E. | There's also the fact that until St Ambrose, reading was always done aloud. He was the first to start reading without forming the words, which caused St Augustine no end of confusion. But why did they read aloud? A letter written in bad handwriting is often easier to decipher that way. I often read aloud when I receive letters from French correspondents, who are the only people in the world who still write their letters by hand.

J.-C. C. | Are we really the only ones?

U. E. | Yes. I've no doubt it's the legacy of a certain type of upbringing. We were advised to do it in my youth, too. A typed letter might be seen as rather too close to commercial correspondence. In other countries they realise that if you want to be read and understood it's best to write legible letters, and that the computer is therefore our best ally. But not the French. The French insist on sending indecipherable handwritten letters. Everywhere else, people have lost not only the habit of writing handwritten letters, but of reading them. In the old days, typesetters could read any handwriting they were presented with.

J.-C. C. | The only thing that is still – usually – handwritten is a doctor's prescription.

U. E. | Pharmacists were invented to decipher them.

J.-C. C. | Whole professions will be lost if handwritten correspondence disappears. Graphologists, public letter-writers, collectors and sellers of autographs . . . What I miss most since computers is the existence of rough drafts. Especially for dialogue scenes. I miss the mistakes, the words scribbled in the margin, the chaos, the arrows pointing all over the place – all those signs of movement, of life, of unresolved searching. And then there's the overview of the whole text. When I write a film scene, which might take six pages to unfold, I like to have the six handwritten pages in front of me to give me a sense of the rhythm; that way any over-long passages are immediately visible. I can't do that on a computer. I have to print the pages and spread them out in front of me. What about you, what do you still write by hand?

U. E. | Notes for my secretary. But that's not all. I always start a novel with handwritten notes. Sketches and diagrams, which are hard to do on a computer.

J.-C. C. | This issue of rough drafts reminds me of when Borges came to visit me, in 1976 or '77. I had just bought my Paris house and we were having a lot of building work done. It was chaos. I collected Borges from his hotel. We arrived and crossed the courtyard, with him holding my arm because he was almost blind. We climbed the stairs and I thoughtlessly decided to apologise for the mess that he obviously could not see. He replied: 'Yes, I understand. It's a draft.' He saw everything – even a building site – through the lens of literature.

U. E. | Speaking of drafts, I'd like to mention a very telling phenomenon linked to the cultural changes brought about by new technology. We use computers, but we print like madmen. I probably print out a ten-page document fifty times, and thus kill a dozen trees, whereas before computers came into my life I might have killed only ten.

The Italian philologist Gianfranco Contini used to practise what he called the critique of *scartafacci* or variants – namely, studying different drafts of a work before it reached its definitive form. How can we do this kind of variant research in an electronic age? Well, what we actually find is that the computer adds rather than cuts down on intermediary stages. I wrote *The Name of the Rose* in the days before I had a word processor, and I used to give someone else my corrected manuscript to retype. I would then correct the new version and give it to them to type out again. But that couldn't go on and on for ever – at a certain point I was forced to settle on the version I held in my hands. I'd had enough.

On the computer, however, I print, correct, put in my corrections, print again, and so it goes on. I do many more drafts. In this way I might correct 200 versions of the same text. The philologist would be totally overworked. And that still wouldn't be the complete series. There's also a phantom version. I write my text A on the computer. Print it out. Correct it by hand. Now we have text B, the corrections for which I input onto my computer. Then I print out again and think (as would the philologists of the future) that what I have is a text C. But actually, it is a text D, because while I was putting the corrections into the computer, I would certainly have taken some spontaneous decisions and made some further changes. Therefore between B and D – between the text I corrected and the corrected version on the computer – there is a phantom version that is the true version C. The same goes for later corrections. The philologists would therefore have to reconstruct as many phantom versions as there are journeys between screen and paper.

J.-C. C. | Fifteen years ago there was a movement of American writers who protested against the computer on the grounds that because early drafts of a text appeared onscreen already in typeface, they possessed an innate authority that made them harder to analyse or correct. The screen gave them the dignity and status of a text that was already almost published. Another school, on the other hand, believed – like you – that the computer offers infinite possibilities for correction and improvement.

U. E. | Of course it does, because the text you see on the screen is already a stranger's text. And thus fair game for critical ferocity.

J.-P. DE T. | Jean-Claude, you just mentioned the papyrus scrolls, or volumina, which were books before the time of books or even codices. That stage of the history of the book is by far the least known.

U. E. | In ancient Rome there used to be shops selling scrolls next to the libraries. A collector could go to the bookseller and order a copy of Virgil, for example. The bookseller would ask him to come back in a fortnight, whereupon the book would have been specially copied out for him. Maybe they stocked a few copies of the most popular titles. We actually know very little about the history of book-buying, even after the advent of the printing press. The first printed books were not sold bound. You had to buy the sheets of paper, and then have the book bound to order. And the variety of bindings is one of the most delightful things about book-collecting. The binding can make a substantial difference between two copies of the same book, for the book lover as much as the antiques dealer. I think the first pre-bound books came on the market between the seventeenth and eighteenth centuries.

J.-C. C. | They are called 'publisher's bindings'.

U. E. | Interior designers buy them up by the yard to put on rich people's bookshelves. But another way to personalise printed books was to leave out the large capital letters on each page so that they could be filled in later by an illuminator, allowing the owner to feel as if he possessed a unique manuscript. This was obviously done by hand. If the book contained illustrations, these would similarly have been touched up by hand.

J.-C. C. | It's also important to remember that books were very expensive then; only kings, princes and rich bankers could afford them. That little incunabulum I showed you was probably worth a lot more when it was made than it is worth now. Just think how many baby calves would have been killed to make a book like that: each page is printed on vellum, which is to say the skin of newborn calves. As Régis Debray asks, what if the Greeks and Romans had been vegetarian? We would have been deprived of the entire legacy of classical literature, because all of it was written on parchment, which is tanned and toughened animal hide.

Those books, then, were very expensive – but from the fifteenth century a few pennies would buy an unbound book printed on cheap paper. Merchants used to hawk these books across the whole of Europe, just as certain scholars would cross the Channel or the Alps to find a particularly rare book that they desperately needed, which was kept in an Italian monastery.

U. E. | You must have heard the lovely story of Gerbert d'Aurillac, otherwise known as the Pope of the year 1000, Sylvester II. The Pope is informed that a certain person in possession of a copy of Lucan's *Pharsalia* is willing to trade it. In exchange, he promises an armillary sphere made of leather. He receives the manuscript and sees that the end is missing. Not knowing that Lucan committed suicide before completing the book, he avenges himself by sending only half the sphere. Gerbert was an erudite scholar, but also a collector. The year 1000 is often portrayed as a Neanderthal era, but this story shows how that was far from the case.

J.-C. C. | It is also far from the case that Africa was devoid of books, or that books have been the mark of Western civilisation in particular. The library at Timbuktu is full of ancient books. Ever since the Middle Ages, students travelling to Mali to meet the country's wise men would bring books with them as currency.

U. E. | I've been to that library. It was always a dream of mine to visit Timbuktu before I died. Which reminds me of a story that may seem to be completely off the point, but which actually says a lot about the power of books. When I went to Mali I had the good fortune to visit the land of the Dogon people, whose cosmology is described by Marcel Griaule in his famous book *Conversations with Ogotemmeli* (1948). Griaule's detractors claimed that he had made most of it up. But if you were to ask an old Dogon about his religion today, he would tell you exactly what Griaule wrote – which is to say that what Griaule wrote has become the Dogon's historical memory.

When you arrive there (or rather *up* there, because it's at the top of a remarkable cliff) you find yourself surrounded by clamouring children. I asked one if he was a Muslim. 'No,' he replied, 'I'm an animist.' But no animist would ever say he was an animist unless he'd studied social sciences at university. An animist by definition cannot know he is one, just as Neanderthal man did not know he was Neanderthal. So here we have an example of an oral culture that has been greatly influenced by books.

But let's return to ancient books. We've said that printed books were mainly read by the highly educated. They were, however, certainly read by a much wider circle of people than the codices or manuscripts that preceded them; one can therefore say without hesitation that the invention of the printing press was a democratic revolution. It's impossible to imagine the Protestant Reformation or the increased influence of the Bible without the support of the printed word. In the sixteenth century, the Venetian printer Aldus Manutius brilliantly created a far more portable book, a kind of paperback. As far as I can tell, a more efficient way of transporting information remains to be found. Even the mega-gigabyte computer still needs to be plugged in. Not a problem with the book. I'll say it again – the book is like the wheel. Once invented, it cannot be bettered.

J.-C. C. | Speaking of the wheel, one of the big questions experts are always trying to resolve is why no pre-Columbian cultures invented it?

U. E. | Perhaps because most of them were located on such steep hillsides that the wheel wouldn't have been much competition for the llama.

J.-C. C. | But Mexico has some massive plains. It's very strange, because they did use wheels in their toys.

U. E. | You probably also know that in the first century BC, King Heron of Alexandria invented many quite remarkable things that remained – as you say – nothing but toys.

J.-C. C. | They say that, to give the gods greater status, he even invented a temple with automatic doors, like the ones we have on our garages today.

U. E. | It was simply that it was easier to have slaves do certain jobs than to bring these inventions into practical use.

J.-C. C. | In Mexico, runners would relay the 250 miles to the sea in order to bring fresh fish to the emperor's table in less than a day. Each runner would sprint 400 or 500 yards and then pass on his cargo. Which confirms your hypothesis.

Let me come back to the spread of books. To this perfect wheel of knowledge, as you call it. It's important to remember that sixteenth- and even fifteenth-century Europe was extremely turbulent, and that those we would call the intellectuals used to exchange frequent letters. They wrote to each other in Latin. And the book was an object that could circulate freely in those difficult times. It was one of the tools for safeguarding culture, just as it was at the end of the Roman Empire when certain intellectuals retreated to monasteries to copy out all they could save of a civilisation they knew was about to collapse. In fact, this always happens, every time a culture is under threat.

It's a shame the film world hasn't acted on this precautionary principle. There is an American book of photographs of lost films. All that remains of those lost films are a few images from which we have to reconstruct the film itself. Rather like the Iranian book-binder.

But there is more. The novelisation of films – by which I mean the adaptation of a film into an illustrated book – is something that has been happening for a very long time. Ever since the silent-film era. We still have some of these film-based books, even though the films themselves have disappeared. The book has survived the film that inspired it. This means that we already have an archaeology of film. And now, here is a question that no one has ever been able to answer for me: could people walk into the Library of Alexandria, sit down and read a book, as I can at the Bibliothèque nationale?

U. E. | I don't know either, and I wonder if anyone does. But first you have to ask yourself how many people even knew how to read. Nor do we know how many books they had in Alexandria. We know more about the medieval libraries, which always contained far fewer books than you might think.

J.-C. C. | Tell me about your collection. How many actual incunabula do you own?

J.-P. DE T. | You've already referred to 'incunabula' quite a few times. We've understood that they are ancient books. But perhaps it's worth being more specific?

U. E. | People often think that an incunabulum is an illuminated manuscript. An Italian journalist once described a library as containing incunabula from the thirteenth century, even though he was a very cultured man . . .

J.-C. C. | When in fact 'incunabula' are all the books published between the invention of printing and the night of 31st December 1500. The Latin word *incunabula* refers to the 'cradle' of the history of the printed book – in other words, all the books printed in the fifteenth century. It is generally thought that the 42-line Gutenberg Bible (which, inconveniently, lacks the printing and production note known as the colophon that was printed on the final pages of ancient books) was printed sometime between 1452 and 1455. The years that followed constituted this 'cradle' – and it has become convention to close this period on the last day of 1500, as the year 1500 still belongs to the fifteenth century. Just as the year 2000 is still part of the twentieth century. Which is why, incidentally, it was quite absurd to celebrate the beginning of the twenty-first century on 31st December 1999. We should have celebrated at the real end of the century, on 31st December 2000. But we discussed all that in *Conversations about the End of Time*.

U. E. | You just have to count it out on your fingers. Ten is part of the first ten. So 100 is part of the first hundred. You have to get to 31st December 1500 – fifteen times 100 – before you start a new hundred. This arbitrary date was fixed out of pure snobbishness, because there's nothing to distinguish a book printed in 1499 from one printed in 1502. Antique dealers who want to make a book printed in 1501 seem more appealing shrewdly call it a 'post-incunabulum'. But, strictly speaking, in those terms even the book that is being produced from our conversations can be called a post-incunabulum.

And now, to reply to your question, I only possess about thirty incunabula, though they do include what you might call the 'essentials'. For instance, the *Hypnerotomachia Poliphili*, the *Nuremberg Chronicle*,

Ficino's translation of the *Corpus Hermeticum*, the *Arbor Vitae Crucifixae Jesu Christi* by Ubertino Da Casale (who became one of the characters in my *Name of the Rose)*, and so on. My collection is very focused. It is a *Bibliotheca Semiologica Curiosa Lunatica Magica et Pneumatica*, or 'a collection dedicated to the occult and mistaken sciences'. For example, I have Ptolemy, who was wrong about the movement of the Earth, but not Galileo, who was right.

J.-C. C. | I'm sure then that you possess the works of Athanasius Kircher, who had the kind of encyclopaedic mind you enjoy and definitely promulgated more than a few mistaken ideas . . .

U. E. | I have all his books except the *Ars Magnesia*, which is impossible to get hold of, despite being a small book with no illustrations. Kircher wasn't yet known at the time of publication, so I expect only a few copies were printed. Also, the book is so devoid of charm that probably no one thought it worth saving. But I also possess the works of Robert Fludd and a fair few other eccentric minds.

J.-P. DE T. | Could you tell us a little about Kircher?

J.-C. C. | He was a seventeenth-century German Jesuit who lived in Rome for many years. He wrote about thirty books on subjects as diverse as mathematics, astronomy, music, sound, archaeology, medicine, China, Latium, volcanology and who knows what else. Some consider him the founding father of Egyptology, despite his interpretation of hieroglyphs being utterly wrong.

U. E. | Still, in finding the key to hieroglyphs, Champollion used not only the Rosetta Stone, but also data published by Kircher. In 1992 I taught a course on the search for a perfect language at the Collège de France, and devoted one of my classes to Athanasius Kircher and his interpretation of hieroglyphs. On the day of that class, the college porter said, 'Watch out, Professor sir. All the Sorbonne Egyptologists are in there, sitting in the front row.' I thought I was completely done for. I was very careful in the lecture not to talk about hieroglyphs in general, but only about Kircher's thinking on the subject. But I needn't have worried: the Egyptologists loved it. I realised they had never explored Kircher's work, having heard him described merely as a madman. I was also lucky enough to meet the Egyptologist Jean Yoyotte, who sent me a fantastic reading list on the loss and rediscovery of the hieroglyphic key. The disappearance of a language such as

that of the ancient Egyptians is obviously of particular interest to us now, as we experience new threats
to the continuance of our culture.

J.-C. C. | Kircher was also the first to publish a sort of ency-
clopaedia about China: *China Monumentis.*

U. E. | He was the first to realise that in Chinese ideograms,
meaning was expressed iconically.

J.-C. C. | Not to mention his excellent *Ars Magna Lucis et
Umbrae,* which contains the first representation of
an eye watching moving images by means of a
revolving disc – making him, theoretically, the
inventor of cinema. People also say that he pioneered
the use of the magic lantern in Europe. So he had
a finger in every field of contemporary knowledge.
One could describe Kircher as a kind of Internet
before its time – meaning that he knew everything
that could be known, and within this knowledge
there was 50 per cent accuracy and 50 per cent
nonsense, or imagination. A proportion that probably isn't far off that of the Internet. I should add
– and this is one of the reasons we love him – that
he also invented the cat piano (one simply pulled
on their tails) and a machine to clean out volcanoes
(he had himself lowered into the smoking crater of

Vesuvius in a large basket controlled by an army of little Jesuits).

But the main reason collectors prize Kircher is the exceptional beauty of his books. I think both of us are Kircher fans – of his most exquisitely produced books at least. I am only missing one, but one of the most important: the *Œdipus Aegyptiacus*, considered one of the most beautiful books in the world.

U. E. | For me the most interesting is the *Arca Noe*, with its several-times-folded plate featuring the bowels of the Ark with all the animals, including the snakes hidden in the depths of the hold.

J.-C. C. | And that amazing plate of the flood. And then there's the *Turris Babel*, in which he uses clever calculations to show that the Tower of Babel could never have been built because, even if it had somehow been finished, it would have been so heavy and tall as to make the Earth revolve on its axis.

U. E. | The plate shows the Earth having revolved, with the tower sticking out horizontally from one side like a male member. Fantastic! I also have the works of one of Kircher's disciples, another German Jesuit called Gaspar Schott – but listen, I don't want to flaunt all my possessions. The interesting question is: what makes a collector gravitate to this or that book? Why do we both collect books by Kircher? There are many factors to consider when choosing a very old book. The pure love of the object, perhaps. A collector might own a nineteenth-century book with uncut pages that they wouldn't cut for love or money. It's a matter of protecting the object for its own sake, keeping it intact. Other collectors are exclusively interested in bindings. They have no interest in the contents of the books they own. Some care only about the publishers, and try to get their hands on everything published by Manuce, for example. Others are passionate about one particular title. They want to own every edition of *The Divine Comedy*. Others focus on a certain field, such as eighteenth-century French literature. Then there are those who build their libraries around a single subject, as is the case with me. As I said, I collect books on wrong, zany and occult science, as well as on imaginary languages.

J.-C. C. | And how do you explain this bizarre choice?

U. E. | I am fascinated by error, by bad faith and idiocy. Like Flaubert. You and I both adore silliness. In *Faith in Fakes* I describe visiting American museums that show reproductions of art works, including a waxwork Venus de Milo with arms. In *The Limits of Interpretation*

I create a theory of fakes and forgeries. With regard to my novels, *Foucault's Pendulum* was inspired by occultists who believe feverishly in everything, whereas the main character in *Baudolino* is a delightful and, in the end, benevolent charlatan.

J.-C. C. | Probably also because the not true is the only possible path to truth.

U. E. | Fakes put all attempts to create a theory of truth into question. If you have access to the authentic work, the source of inspiration, then it's possible to ascertain whether or not something is a fake. It is much harder to prove that an authentic work is authentic.

J.-C. C. | I am not a proper collector. I have just always bought books because I like them. My favourite thing in a library is juxtaposition: different books clashing with and contradicting each other.

U. E. | Like you, my neighbour in Milan only collects books that he finds beautiful. So he might have a Vitruvius, an incunabulum of *The Divine Comedy* and a beautiful book of contemporary art. I'm the opposite. I've mentioned my passion for Kircher – I would be willing to pay a fortune to acquire his *Ars Magnesia*, which is the plainest of them all, and thus to own all his books.

Incidentally, it turns out that this neighbour and I both own a copy of the *Hypnerotomachia Poliphili,* or *Poliphilo's Strife of Love in a Dream* – possibly the most beautiful book in the world. We laugh because, right across from our building, the famous Castello Sforzesco library contains a third copy of this same *Hypnerotomachia,* so our little spot has without question the highest concentration of *Hypnerotomachiae* anywhere in the world! I am of course referring to the first incunable edition published in 1499, not subsequent editions.

J.-C. C. | Are you still adding to your collection?

U. E. | I used to trek around all over the world digging up interesting bits and pieces. But I don't do that so much any more. I aim for quality. Or else I try to fill gaps in an author's *opera omnia,* as with Kircher.

J.-C. C. | The collector's mania is often more to get his hands on a rare object than actually to retain it. Let me tell you a great anecdote. There still existed two copies of the founding book of Brazilian literature, *The Guarani* (published in Rio around 1840). One was in a museum; the other was lingering somewhere indeterminate. My friend, the great Brazilian collector José Mindlin, heard that this second copy was in the possession of someone in Paris who was prepared to sell. He was so determined to meet the owner of the coveted book that he took a flight from Rio and a room at the Paris Ritz. The two men spent three intense days at the Ritz haggling and negotiating. Eventually, they reached an agreement and the book became the property of José Mindlin, who took the plane straight back to Brazil. During the flight he had time to explore his recent acquisition, and was rather vexed to find that the book itself was not particularly remarkable. He examined it minutely, looking for the rare details, the peculiarities, and then put it down next to him. When the flight landed he accidentally left it on the plane. He had acquired the object, but the object had, at the same time, lost all importance. He was actually very lucky, because the Air France staff had noticed the book and kept it aside, so he was able to get it back. He said that in the end it hadn't meant much to him. Which I can confirm – I didn't find it particularly painful when I once lost part of my library.

U. E. | That's happened to me, too. The true collector is more concerned with the search than with the eventual ownership, just as the true hunter is interested first in the chase and only afterwards in the preparation and eating of the animals he has killed. I have

134

known collectors (and remember that people collect all sorts of things – books, stamps, postcards, champagne corks . . .) who have spent their entire life assembling an exhaustive collection only to sell it once it's complete, or even give it to a library or museum . . .

J.-C. C. | Like you, I am sent a great many booksellers' catalogues. Most of these are catalogues of catalogues of books. 'Books on books' as they are known. And certain auctions sell nothing but bookshop catalogues – some of them from the eighteenth century.

U. E. | Those catalogues are real works of art in themselves, but I have to get rid of them. As we shall discuss, space for books is too valuable. These days I take almost all the catalogues to the university, where I'm running a Master's programme for budding editors and publishers. It includes a class on the history of the book. I keep only a few, on subjects dear to my heart, or else because they're terribly handsome. Some of these catalogues aren't designed for proper book lovers, but simply for wealthy people who want to invest in old books. They look almost like art books, and would cost a fortune if they weren't sent out for free.

J.-P. DE T. | I can't help asking what these incunabula cost. Does the fact that you each own several mean that you are seriously rich?

U. E. | It depends. These days there are incunabula that cost millions of euros, and others that can be bought for just a few hundred. For a collector, part of the pleasure is in paying half or a quarter of the value of a very rare book that you've managed to unearth. As the market shrinks, that's becoming less and less common, but it still isn't completely impossible to find the occasional bargain. Sometimes a book lover can even buy something for a decent price from a supposedly expensive antiques dealer. In America, a book in Latin won't interest the collectors even if it's terribly rare, because they don't read foreign languages, and definitely not Latin; that's even more the case if the major academic libraries already have a copy. American collectors would be far more thrilled by a Mark Twain first edition, for instance (at any price). I once found Francesco Giorgi's wonderful *De Harmonia Mundi,* published in 1525, at the highly reputed New York dealer Kraus, which sadly closed a few years ago. I had seen a copy in Milan, but thought it too expensive. The big academic libraries already had the book and so, because for the average American collector a book in Latin is completely devoid of interest, I was able to buy it at Kraus for one-fifth of the price asked in Milan.

I once got a bargain in Germany, too. I was browsing through the catalogue for an auction selling thousands of books categorised into sections. I happened to look at the books under the title 'Theology', and suddenly saw the title *Offenbarung göttlicher Mayestat* by Aloysius Gutman. Gutman, Gutman . . . I knew that name from somewhere. I did a bit of research and found out that Gutman is considered the inspiration behind all the Rosicrucian manifestos, but that his book had never appeared in a catalogue on the subject, at least not for the last thirty years. It was being auctioned for an initial asking price of 100 euros in today's money. I hoped it might escape the attention of collectors as it should really have been in the 'Occult' section. The auction was to take place in Munich. I wrote to my German editor (who's based in Munich) and asked him to announce his intention to buy, but not to go over 200 euros. He got it for 150.

Not only is the book hugely rare, it also has red, black and green Gothic script notes in the margin of every page, which are a work of art in themselves. However, apart from flukes of that kind, auctions have become exorbitant over the last few years on account of new buyers who know nothing about books, but have simply been told that buying old books is a good investment. Which is utter rubbish. If you buy gilts for 1,000 pounds, you can sell them a short time later for either the same price or some kind of profit, by simply telephoning your bank. But if you buy a book for 1,000 pounds, you won't be able to sell it for 1,000 pounds tomorrow. The bookseller needs to clear a profit too: he has incurred costs relating to the catalogue, his shop, and so on, and will in any case usually try to fob you off with less than a quarter of the book's market value. Furthermore, it will take him a little while to find the right buyer. The only time you will make any money is after you die, if your book collection is sold off at Christie's.

Five or six years ago, a Milanese book dealer showed me a superb Ptolemy incunabulum. Unfortunately he was asking the equivalent of 100,000 euros. Too expensive – for me at any rate. If I had bought it, it is very unlikely that I would have found any way to resell it for that kind of price. And yet three weeks later, a similar Ptolemy was sold at public auction for 700,000 euros. So-called investors were having a great time bidding each other up. What's more – and I've been checking – each time the book has subsequently appeared in a catalogue it has been offered for at least that price. Real collectors will never get their hands on the book at prices like that.

J.-C. C. | It becomes a financial object, a product, and that's sad. Real collectors, genuine book lovers, do not tend to be enormously rich. As with everything, when books become bankable and labelled as 'investments', something is lost.

U. E. | First of all, collectors don't attend the auctions. These auctions take place all over the world, and one would need substantial funds simply to attend them all. But the other reason is that the booksellers have literally taken over the market: they agree amongst themselves not to drive up the prices, and then meet at the hotel to redistribute what they have bought. You might have to wait ten years to get your hands on a coveted book. Another of my best bargains was from Kraus. They were selling five identically bound incunabula for a price that was of course much higher than I could afford. Every time I went back, they still hadn't sold the books, so I would tease them that they must be selling too high. In the end, the boss said he wanted to reward my obstinacy and determination, and sold me the books for about half what he had previously been asking. A month later, I saw in another catalogue that a single one of those incunabula had been valued at approximately double what I had paid for all five. And over the following years, the price of each of the five has continued to rise. Ten years of patience. It's great sport.

J.-C. C. | Do you think that people will always have a taste for very old books? Top booksellers are rather concerned about this, because their profession is done for, if the customers are nothing but bankers. Several booksellers I know have told me that there are fewer and fewer genuine book lovers among the younger generations.

U. E. | It's important to remember that ancient books are by their very nature an endangered species. If I were to own a very rare jewel, or even a Raphael, my family would sell it when I died. But if I had created a great library, I would generally have specified in my will that I did not want it dispersed, because I had spent my whole life piecing it together. So either it would be given to a public institution or sold via Christie's to a large, usually American, library.

These books thus vanish definitively from the market. The diamond is back on the market each time its new owner dies. But the incunabulum is henceforth accredited to the Boston library catalogue.

J.-C. C. | Never again to depart.

U. E. | Never. Therefore, over and above the damage done by so-called investors, each copy of an ancient book becomes progressively more rare, and therefore more expensive. As for the younger generations, I do not think that the taste for rare books has been lost. It seems to me that it has actually never existed, as the price of ancient books has always been more than what young people can afford. Although I must say that if someone is really keen they can create a good collection without spending too much. I recently found two sixteenth-century books by Aristotle that I had bought casually as a young man; the bookseller's pencilled price on the title page shows that they cost me something like two euros in today's money. From an antiquarian bookseller's point of view, that's pretty cheap.

A friend of mine collects the little BUR (Biblioteca Universale Rizzoli) books, which are the equivalent of the German Reclam collection. These books were published in the 1950s and have become extremely rare because they looked so humble and cost so little that no one thought to take good care of them. Piecing together the entire collection of almost a thousand titles is a fascinating endeavour, which doesn't require a lot of money or any dealings with expensive antique dealers, just a thorough ransacking of flea markets (or these days, eBay). So you can be a cut-price bibliophile. Another friend of mine collects good-value old (but not necessarily first) editions of his favourite poets because he says that reading poems in a period edition 'tastes' better.

But does that make him a bibliophile? Or simply a poetry enthusiast? There are second-hand bookstalls and markets all over the place, where you can track down nineteenth-century books and even twentieth-century first editions for the price of a cheap meal (unless you want a first edition of *Les Fleurs du Mal*). A student of mine used to collect out-of-date tourist guides to different cities, which he bought for next to nothing. He then used them to create his thesis on the appearance of a city over several decades. After that he published the thesis as a book.

J.-C. C. | Let me tell you how I came to own a one-of-a-kind set of the complete works of Fludd, all in the same period binding. The story starts with a rich English family, their impressive library and their several children. As often happens, only one of the children recognised the true value of the books. When the father died, the connoisseur said to his brothers and sisters: 'I want only the books. You can have the rest.' The others were delighted. They had the land, the money, the furniture and the house. But the new owner could not sell the books on the open market in case his family found out and realised that 'only the books' was not 'only' at all, and that they had been conned. So he decided to sell them covertly to international brokers, who are often very odd characters indeed. The

Fludd came to me via a broker who used to go round on a moped, carting these treasures with him in a plastic bag on his handlebars. It took me four years to pay for the set. None of the owner's family ever found out who ended up with all those well-travelled books, or how much they paid.

Books with a will to survive

J.-P. DE T. | It seems that you have sometimes taken the most extraordinary trouble to track down a particular book – whether to complete an author series, enrich your specialist collection, out of simple love for a beautiful object or because of what the book means to you personally. Perhaps you could share some stories about this painstaking detective work?

J.-C. C. | There was the time I went to see the director of the National Archives, about fifteen years ago. Now it's important to remember that in France – as in every country with a national archive – a truck arrives every day to take away a heap of old papers that are to be thrown out. Filtering and destruction occur here, too; that's just the way of the world.

Before the truck arrives, they sometimes give people who collect old papers such as legal documents and marriage contracts access to what is about to be destroyed. The director told me a story about coming to work one day just as one of those trucks was leaving. Now this is a great example of the 'eagle eye', the eye that has learned how to see and is waiting for just this chance. Anyway, she moves aside to let the truck pass and suddenly notices the edge of a piece of yellowing paper sticking out of a huge bundle. She stops the truck, has a cable undone and the relevant bundle opened, and finds one of the few known posters from Molière's Illustre Théâtre at the time when it was performing outside Paris. How had the poster ended up there? And why was it about to be burned? How many precious documents and rare books have been destroyed as a result of simple negligence, oversight or accident? Perhaps carelessness has caused even more damage than intentional destruction.

U. E. | A collector needs the 'eagle eye' that you've just described. I went to Granada a few months ago. Once I'd seen the Alhambra and all the other things you're supposed to see, I asked a friend to take me to an antiquarian bookshop. It was unusually chaotic and I was rummaging rather fruitlessly through a huge pile of Spanish books that held absolutely no interest for me when, suddenly, my eye was drawn to two books. I had happened upon two Spanish books on mnemonics. I bought one, and the bookseller gave me the other. You might say this was simple good luck and that there must have been other treasures in that bookshop, but I am sure there weren't. It's a kind of canine instinct that leads you straight to your prey.

J.-C. C. | I sometimes visit second-hand bookshops with my friend, the wonderful author and well-known bookseller

148

Gérard Oberlé. He walks into the shop, looks through the shelves very slowly and suddenly picks up *the* book that was meant for him. Most recently it was a very rare first edition of Samuel Beckett's book on Proust. I also knew a superb bookseller in the rue de l'Université, who specialised in scientific books and objects. When I was a student he would let me and my friends into his shop even though he knew that we wouldn't be able to buy anything. But he talked to us, and showed us his beautiful things. He was a major influence on my tastes. He lived on the rue du Bac, on the other side of boulevard Saint-Germain. One night he was walking home up the rue du Bac. He crossed the boulevard and, as he was walking along, he noticed a small piece of brass poking out of a rubbish bin. He stopped, lifted the lid, went through the bin and pulled out one of the twelve calculators made by Pascal himself. Absolutely priceless. It now lives in the National Conservatory of Arts and Crafts, the CNAM. Who had thrown it out? And such synchronicity, that this eagle eye happened to be there at that precise moment.

U. E. | I had to laugh just now, when I told you about my great find in the Granada bookshop – if I'm honest, I am not at all sure that he didn't have a third book I would have found just as fascinating as the other two. And maybe your bookseller friend walked past an object meant for him three times without seeing it, and only noticed Pascal's calculator on the fourth pass.

J.-C. C. | One of the earliest texts in the Catalan language dates from the thirteenth century. The two-page manuscript disappeared a long time ago, but a printed version from the fifteenth century still exists. This is therefore an extremely rare incunabulum. For a Catalan collector, it is clearly the most precious book in the world. I happen to know a Barcelonan bookseller who searched for this document for years, like a dogged detective on a cold trail. He eventually unearthed the precious text, bought it and sold it on to the Barcelona library for a price he has never revealed, but that I'm sure was extremely impressive.

A few years passed. Then one day the same bookseller bought a large eighteenth-century folio whose binding was stuffed with old papers, as is often the case. So he did what you do in such a situation, and carefully slit the binding with a razor, so that the papers fell out. Among these old papers was the thirteenth-century manuscript that had supposedly been lost for years. The genuine original manuscript. He nearly fainted. Here was the actual treasure. Waiting for him. Whoever slipped it in there clearly hadn't had the faintest idea what they were doing.

U.E. | Quaritch is the best antiquarian bookseller in England, and perhaps the world. The company once organised an exhibition and catalogue of manuscripts found inside bindings. They even had a meticulous description of a manuscript that had survived the library fire in *The Name of the Rose,* the manuscript being of course completely invented. I noticed (a simple check of the measurements showed that it was the size of a postage stamp) and we became firm friends. But lots of people thought it was a genuine document.

J.-C. C. | Do you think there's any possibility that a new play by Sophocles could still be found?

U.E. | There was recently a massive Italian controversy about a papyrus scroll by the Greek geographer Artemidorus, which Turin's San Paolo Bank Foundation had bought for a fortune. The two top Italian experts disagreed as to whether the text was genuine or a fake. Every day the newspapers featured a sensational statement by some new expert, confirming or contradicting the previous day's coverage. All this is to say that relics of lesser or greater value do still pop up every now and then. The Dead Sea Scrolls were only rediscovered fifty years ago. It seems to me that we're more likely to unearth these kinds of documents today, with all the building work going on and thus all the disruption of the soil. There's a greater probability of finding a Sophocles manuscript now than in Schliemann's day.

J.-P. DE T. | As book lovers, what would be your dearest wish? What would you most like to see re-emerge from the earth of a building site?

U. E. | I'd like to dig up and keep, selfishly, a copy of the Gutenberg Bible, the first book ever printed. I'd also love them to find the lost plays that Aristotle discusses in his *Poetics*. Other than that, I do not feel the absence of many lost books. Perhaps because, as we have said, they probably disappeared for a reason – maybe they weren't worth saving from the fire or the inquisition that destroyed them.

J.-C. C. | For my part, I would be thrilled to discover an unknown Mayan codex. When I visited Mexico for the first time, in 1964, I was told that they knew of the existence of a few hundred thousand pyramids, but that only 300 had been excavated. Years later I asked an archaeologist working at Palenque how much longer the dig would go on. He replied, 'About five hundred and fifty years.' The pre-Columbian world probably suffered the grimmest attempt at total cultural destruction – at wiping out every trace of a language, a means of expression, a literature and therefore a way of thinking. As if the conquered peoples did not deserve to be remembered in any way. Piles of codices were burned in the Yucatan under the orders of a few Christian fanatics. In the case of the Aztecs as well as the Mayans, barely a handful of copies survived, and those only in remarkable circumstances. One Mayan codex was spotted by a nineteenth-century 'eagle eye', just as it was about to be burned in a Paris fireplace.

Having said that, the ancient languages of the Americas are not dead. They are even undergoing a renaissance. Nahuatl, the language of the Aztecs, has laid its claim to be the national language of Mexico. *Waiting for Godot* has just been translated into Nahuatl – I've already ordered a first edition.

J.-P. DE T. | Is it conceivable that a completely unheard-of book might still be discovered?

J.-C. C. | Now here's a truly remarkable story. The main character is Paul Pelliot, a young French linguist and explorer at the beginning of the twentieth century. Pelliot was a highly gifted linguist, a little like Champollion a century before, and an archaeologist to boot. He and a German team were exploring one of the silk roads in the Dunhuang region of western China. Thanks to the caravans travelling the region, we have long known that Dunhuang contains caves filled with statues of the Buddha and many other relics.

In 1911, Pelliot and his colleagues discovered a cave that had been walled up since the tenth century AD. They negotiated with the Chinese government for it to be opened. The cave turned out to contain 70,000 manuscripts, all from before the tenth century. Some say this was the greatest archaeological find of the twentieth century. A whole cave of unknown books! Pelliot – and his was an eagle eye if ever there was one – must have been ecstatic; this was akin to suddenly being given access to a secret room in the Library of Alexandria, in which everything had been preserved. How his heart must have raced. There's a photo of him sitting among piles of antique texts, reading them by candlelight. Feeling incredibly blessed, we can be sure.

He lived in the cave among the treasures for three weeks, starting to categorise them. He discovered two lost languages, including the ancient Pahlavi, an Old Persian language. He also discovered the only Manichaean text we know of that was written (in Chinese) by the Manichaeans themselves rather than by their enemies. My wife Nahal wrote her thesis on that document. In it, Mani is called the 'Buddha of Light'. Pelliot found many other incredible documents too, from all kinds of traditions. He managed to persuade the French government to purchase about 20,000 of these manuscripts from the Chinese. They now form the Pelliot collection at the Bibliothèque nationale, and are still being translated and studied.

J.-P. DE T. | That brings us to another question: is it conceivable that an unknown masterpiece might still be discovered?

U. E. | An Italian aphorist once wrote that there is no such thing as a great Bulgarian poet. This may seem a little racist. What he probably meant was one of two things (and he could have chosen any small country instead of Bulgaria), or perhaps both: firstly, even if this great poet had existed, his language wouldn't have been widely enough known for us to have ever come across his work. So if 'great' means famous, he might be a very good poet, but not famous. When I visited Georgia, they told me that their national poem, Shota Rustaveli's *The Knight in the Panther's Skin,* was a great masterpiece. I agree, but he's hardly caused the same stir as Shakespeare.

Secondly, a country must have endured the great

events of history if it is to produce a mind capable of thinking in a universal way.

J.-C. C. | How many Hemingways were born in Paraguay? When they were born they may have had the potential to produce a work of great originality and power, but they didn't do it. They couldn't. Either they didn't know how to write, or there weren't any editors to support their work, or perhaps they didn't even know that they could write, that they could be 'an author'.

U. E. | In his *Poetics*, Aristotle mentions at least twenty plays that we no longer have. The real issue is this: why did only the works of Sophocles and Euripides survive? Were they the best, the most deserving of posthumous recognition? Or was it that their authors connived to obtain the approval of their peers or to exclude their competitors, precisely the ones that Aristotle mentions because they were the authors that history ought to have retained?

J.-C. C. | Don't forget that some of Sophocles' works have also been lost. Were the lost works of higher quality than those that survived? Perhaps the ones that we still have were those most prized by the Athenian public, which doesn't necessarily make them the most interesting, at least to us. A contemporary reader might prefer the others. Who decided to preserve, or not to preserve, or to translate into Arabic this book rather than that one? How many great authors have we never read? And some of them are very famous, despite us having no access to their work. This brings us back to the concept of the phantom or ghost. Who knows? The greatest writer is perhaps the one whose works we haven't read. Greatness brings anonymity. I'm thinking of those pointless ramblings about who really wrote the works of Shakespeare, or Molière. What does it matter? The real Shakespeare has disappeared into Shakespeare's reputation. Shakespeare would be no one without his work. Shakespeare's works without Shakespeare would remain the works of Shakespeare.

U. E. | Perhaps there's another way of looking at this. Over time, every book is overlaid with all the interpretations that have been made of it. We don't read the same Shakespeare that Shakespeare wrote. Our Shakespeare is much richer than the Shakespeare that was read at the time. A masterpiece isn't a masterpiece until it is well known and has absorbed all the interpretations to which it has given rise, which in turn make it what it is. An unknown masterpiece hasn't had enough readers, or readings, or interpretations. In that sense, one could say that it was the Talmud that gave rise to the Bible.

J.-C. C. | Naturally every reading affects the book, in the same way as the events we experience affect us. A great book is always alive; it grows and ages alongside us, without ever dying. Time enriches and alters it. Mediocre books on the other hand are unaffected by history, and simply disappear. A few years ago I found myself rereading Racine's *Andromache*. I suddenly came across a monologue in which Andromache is telling her servant about the Trojan massacre: 'Think, think, Cephise, of that cruel night / that was for an entire people an endless night.' Since Auschwitz, those lines read differently. The young Racine was already describing genocide.

U. E. | That's what Borges is saying in *Pierre Menard*. He imagines that an author has tried to rewrite *Don Quixote* by immersing himself in seventeenth-century Spanish history and culture. He therefore writes a *Quixote* absolutely identical to the book written by Cervantes, word for word, except that the meaning is different, because a sentence written today doesn't mean the same thing it did then. And we read it differently, too, because the infinite readings that the sentence has provoked have been assimilated into the original text.

158

The unknown masterpiece, on the other hand, has not benefited from that journey.

J.-C. C. | A work of art isn't created a masterpiece, it becomes one. It's important to add that great books have a reciprocal effect on each other through their readers. We can of course explain the great influence that Cervantes had on Kafka. But we can also, as Gerard Genette has conclusively shown, say that Kafka has had an influence on Cervantes. If I read Kafka before reading Cervantes, then through me and without my knowing it, Kafka will impact on my reading of *Quixote*. Just as our journey through life, our personal experiences, the time in which we live, the knowledge we imbibe, everything, even our domestic problems and our children's misfortunes, all of it has an impact on our reading of old books.

I sometimes like to open a book at random. A month ago I had a look at the final, least-read part of *Don Quixote*. Returning from his 'island', Sancho meets an old friend, the converted Moor Ricote, who by royal decree is about to be sent back to Berbery in Africa – a country he doesn't know, with a language he doesn't speak and a religion he doesn't practise, having (like his parents) been born in Spain and thinking himself a good Christian. It's an astonishing page. The character speaks simply and directly to us about ourselves: 'nowhere do we find the haven our misfortune longs for'. That's the authority, the familiarity and the relevance of a great work of literature: we open it, and it speaks to us of ourselves. Because people have been alive since that time, because our experiences have added to and become part of the book.

U. E. | It's the same with the *Mona Lisa*. Personally I find some of da Vinci's other paintings more beautiful, for example *Virgin of the Rocks* and *Lady with an Ermine*. But the *Mona Lisa* has been the object of so many interpretations, and they have settled on the canvas like layers of sediment, and transformed it. T.S. Eliot has already said all this in his essay on *Hamlet*. *Hamlet* is not a masterpiece; it's a muddled tragedy, which fails to bring its disparate sources into a coherent whole. But that's also why it has become an enigma that continues to fascinate and provoke debate all over the world. *Hamlet* isn't a masterpiece on account of its literary qualities; it has become one precisely because it resists our interpretation. Sometimes it's the weirdness that makes a text go down in history.

J.-C. C. | And then there are the rediscoveries. A work may wait a long time before having its hour of glory. I was asked if I would like to adapt *Old Goriot* for TV. I hadn't read the novel in at least thirty years, so I sat down one evening to flick through it. I couldn't put it down until I finished it at three or four in the morning. The pages had such pace and the writing such energy that I couldn't tear my eyes away for a moment. How is it that Balzac, an unmarried, childless man of thirty-two, was able to dissect the relationship between an old father and his daughters with such insight, precision and ruthlessness? For example, Goriot tells his boarding-house companion Rastignac about going to the Champs-Elysées every evening to watch his daughters parade up and down. He has provided them with horse-drawn carriages, footmen and whatever they might need to be happy. He, of course, has become poorer in the process – bankrupt, even. He doesn't want to embarrass them, so he makes sure he isn't seen, and certainly doesn't wave. He merely listens to the admiring remarks made by people watching them go by, and tells Rastignac, 'I envy the little dog on their lap.' What a line! So, there are not only public rediscoveries, but also precious personal rediscoveries made, one evening, when we pick up a forgotten book.

U. E. | I remember as a young man coming across Georges de La Tour, falling in love with his work and not being able to understand why he wasn't considered a genius in the same league as Caravaggio. Decades later, La

Tour was rediscovered and praised to the skies. He became very mainstream. Sometimes all it takes is an exhibition (or a new edition of a book) to stimulate such popularity.

J.-C. C. | While we're at it, we should talk about certain books that have resisted destruction. We've already discussed how the Spanish behaved towards the Amerindian civilisations. All that remains of those literatures are three Mayan and four Aztec codices. The rediscovery of two of these was miraculous: the Mayan codex in Paris, and an Aztec codex now known as the *Codex Florentino* in Florence. Could it be that there are certain stubborn, wily books that were absolutely determined to survive so that we could read them?

J.-P. DE T. | It must be tempting for people with a good idea of their worth to misappropriate precious manuscripts and books. A Bibliothèque nationale librarian was recently accused of stealing a manuscript belonging to the Hebrew collection he managed.

U. E. | Some books have only survived thanks to thieves. This reminds me of Girolamo Libri, a nineteenth-century Florentine count and great mathematician who became a French citizen. This highly respected, erudite scholar was made Special Commissioner for the recovery of manuscripts belonging to the national heritage. He travelled all over France, from monastery to municipal library, saving valuable documents and many precious books from a sad fate. The country that had given him citizenship celebrated this work, until the day they discovered that he had taken thousands of priceless documents and books for his own use. He was threatened with legal proceedings. The entire French intelligentsia of the time, from Guizot to Mérimée, signed a petition defending poor Girolamo Libri and insisting fervently on his integrity. Italian intellectuals protested too. There was unwavering support for this poor, unjustly accused man. They continued to defend him even when the thousands of documents he was accused of having stolen were found at his home. He was probably rather like those Europeans who, having discovered objects in Egypt, thought it quite normal to take them home. Unless of course he was keeping the documents at home until he had categorised them. Girolamo Libri went into exile in England to avoid prosecution, and died there with his reputation in tatters. But no information has come to light since to prove whether or not he was guilty.

J.-P. DE T. | We've talked about books we know existed, but that no one has ever seen or read; unknown masterpieces that will remain for ever unknown; priceless manuscripts stolen or mouldering in a cave for a thousand years. But what about books whose authorship is suddenly put into question, and attributed to another? Did Shakespeare really write Shakespeare? Was Homer really Homer? Etc . . .

J.-C. C. | I've an interesting story about Shakespeare. I happened to be in Beijing just after the Cultural Revolution. I was reading *China Today* in English as I ate my breakfast at the hotel. Of the seven columns on the front page of that morning's paper, five were devoted to a sensational event: specialists in England had just discovered that some of Shakespeare's plays weren't actually written by Shakespeare. I hurriedly scanned the article, only to find that a very few verses scattered among several plays were at issue, and not even interesting ones at that.

That evening I had dinner with two sinologists, and told them how surprised I was. How could a piece of non-news about Shakespeare occupy almost the whole front page of *China Today*? One of them replied, 'You mustn't forget that you're in the land of the Mandarins, where writing has always been linked to power, and is thus of utmost importance. When something happens to the greatest writer in the West or perhaps the whole world, of course that's worth five columns of the front page.'

U. E. | There is an infinite number of studies seeking to confirm or dispute the authenticity of Shakespeare's work. I have collected quite a few, at least of the most famous. The debate goes by the name of 'The Shakespeare–Bacon controversy'. I once wrote a spoof suggesting that if all Shakespeare's works had been written by Bacon, then Bacon would never have had the time to write his own – which must then have been written by Shakespeare.

J.-C. C. | As we've already discussed, we have the same issue in France with regard to Corneille and Molière. Who wrote the works of Molière? Who, if not Molière? When I was studying classics, a lecturer kept us wondering about the 'Homeric Question' for four months. His conclusion was as follows: 'We now know that the Homeric poems were probably written not by Homer, but by his grandson, who was also called Homer.' Things have moved on since then, because experts now agree that *The Iliad* and *The Odyssey* were definitely not written by the same author. The grandson option seems to have been definitively abandoned.

In any case, the notion of a Molière–Corneille collaboration brings to mind all sorts of weird scenarios. Molière ran a theatre, with employees, a stage manager, actors and constant meetings. There are diaries listing his activities as well as the takings of the company. The heart of the matter must therefore have been hidden; Corneille, wrapped in a long black cloak, must have brought him the texts in the dead of night. It would seem extraordinary that no one noticed at the time. But in the absurd world of conspiracy, gullibility has the edge over plausibility. Some people cannot accept the world as it is; being unable to change it, they feel obliged to rewrite it instead.

U.E. | We love the act of creation to be shrouded in mystery. The public demands it. If that weren't the case, how would Dan Brown make a living? We have understood since Charcot why hysterics have stigmata, but we nonetheless persist in idolising Padre Pio. It is boring for Corneille to just be Corneille. Much more interesting for Corneille to be not only Corneille, but Molière as well.

J.-C. C. | In the case of Shakespeare, it's important to remember that very few of his plays were published during his lifetime. It was a long time after his death, in 1623, that they were collected together and published in what is now called the *Folio* and considered the first edition. The holy of holies, naturally. Do any copies of that edition still exist, I wonder?

U.E. | I have seen three at the Folger Library in Washington. There are others in existence, but no longer on the antiquarian book market. There's a story of a bookseller and the 1623 Folio in my *The Mysterious Flame of Queen Loana.* That's every collector's fantasy: getting your hands on the Gutenberg Bible or the 1623 Folio. But there aren't any copies of the Gutenberg Bible on the market any more, as we have said – they are all in the big libraries now. I've seen two of them at the Pierpont Morgan Library in New York, and one of those was incomplete. I touched a vellum copy at the Vatican Library; all the initial letters were hand-coloured. If the Vatican is not Italy, then there isn't a single Gutenberg Bible in the whole of Italy. The last known copy in the world was sold to a Japanese bank twenty years ago for, if I remember rightly, three or four million of the dollars of the time. If another ever emerged, no one has any idea how much it might fetch. Every collector dreams of coming across an old lady with a copy of the Gutenberg Bible stashed away in some cupboard. The lady is ninety-five years old and not in the best of health. The collector offers her 200,000 euros; an enormous sum that will allow her to live out the rest of her days in comfort. But there's an immediate dilemma: what do you do with the Bible once you get it home? Either you don't mention it to anyone, which is a bit like going to a funny film all by yourself – not much fun. Or else you start telling people, and all the thieves in the world spring into action. You don't know what to do, so you take it to the local town hall. It is kept in a safe place and you and your friends can visit it as often as you like. But you aren't able to get up in the middle of the night and stroke it. So what is the point of having your very own Gutenberg Bible?

J.-C. C. | Exactly. What's the point? I have another dream, or daydream. I am a thief, and I sneak into a private house that contains a magnificent collection of ancient books. I've brought a bag, but it will only hold ten books; perhaps another two or three in the pockets. So I have to choose. I open up the bookshelves. I have ten or twelve minutes in which to choose, as the alarm system may already have alerted the police . . . I love that scenario. Violating the private, protected space of a collector whom I imagine rich, paradoxically ignorant and definitely unpleasant. So unpleasant that he will occasionally cut up an extremely rare book to sell it sheet by sheet. A friend of mine obtained a page of a Gutenberg Bible that way.

168

U. E. | If I were to butcher some of my illustrated books in that way, I would make a hundred times what I paid for them.

J.-C. C. | People who cut up books to sell the plates are called scrap dealers. They are the sworn enemies of book lovers worldwide.

U. E. | I knew a New York bookseller who wouldn't sell ancient books any other way. He used to say, 'What I do is democratic vandalism. I buy incomplete copies and break them up. You could never buy a copy of the *Nuremberg Chronicle*, could you? Well, I'll sell you a page for ten dollars.' But did he really only break up incomplete copies? We will never know, and anyway he's dead. There is a sort of agreement between collectors and booksellers whereby collectors promise not to buy single pages and booksellers promise not to sell them. But what about plates that have been separated from their (now-vanished) books for 100 or 200 years? How could one resist a gorgeous framed image? I own a superb colour map by Vincenzo Coronelli. Where did it come from? I don't know.

Our knowledge of the past comes from halfwits, fools and people with a grudge

J.-P. DE T. | Do your collections of antiquarian books enable you to enter into some sort of dialogue with the past? Do you think of them as bearing witness to the time in which they were written?

U. E. | As I've said, I only collect books relating to falsities and mistakes, so they are hardly reliable witnesses. And yet despite lying, these books do have something to teach us about the past.

J.-C. C. | Let's try to imagine a highly educated man of the fifteenth century. He owns 100 or 200 books, some of which may now be in our possession. He has also hung five or six rather inaccurate prints of Jerusalem and Rome on his walls. His sense of the world is hazy, as of something far away. This man would need to travel in order to really get to know the world. Books are beautiful but inadequate and, as you say, often misleading.

U. E. | The *Nuremberg Chronicle* – an illustrated history of the world from Creation to the 1490s – sometimes uses the same plate to represent different cities. It shows us how printers often prioritised illustration over information.

J.-C. C. | My wife and I have built up a collection one could entitle 'Persian Journeys', which includes some books written in the seventeenth century. One of the best known and earliest (dated 1686) is by Jean Chardin. Volume nine contains a foldout of the Persepolis ruins, which must be three metres long unfolded. Engraved plates were stuck one onto the next – and that would have been done for every copy of the book. An inconceivable amount of work.

The same text was reprinted again in the eighteenth century with exactly the same plates. And then again 100 years later, as if Persia hadn't undergone a single change in those 200 years. France had changed, but in books Persia hadn't – as if it was fixed in a certain series of images for ever; an editor's decision had become a judgement on civilisation and on history. Until the nineteenth century, France was publishing as scientific books works that had been written and published 200 years before.

U. E. | It is sometimes the books that are at fault. But sometimes it's our own errors and misinterpretations. In the Sixties I wrote a spoof (published in *Misreadings)* in which a future civilisation finds a titanium box buried in a lake. The box contains documents that Bertrand Russell had put in a safe place at a time when he was organising anti-nuclear marches and we were

174

literally obsessed with the threat of nuclear destruction. Much more obsessed than today, not because the threat has diminished – on the contrary – but because we've become used to it. The joke was that the rescued documents were actually song lyrics. The philologists of the future were therefore trying to reconstruct our vanished civilisation from these songs, which were seen as the high point of our poetic output.

I later heard that my text had been discussed in a Greek philology seminar; the academics were wondering whether the fragments of Greek poetry they were working on weren't somewhat the same.

And actually it's never a good idea to try to reconstruct the past from a single source. What's more, the passage of time renders some texts impossible to understand, as this lovely story shows. About twenty years ago, NASA or some other American government agency was trying to decide where exactly to bury the nuclear waste that, as we know, remains radioactive for 10,000 years or something astronomical. Their problem was that even if they did find suitable land, how could they warn the people of the future not to enter it?

Because after all, over the last 2,000 or 3,000 years we've lost the ability to decipher several languages. If in 5,000 years' time, human beings have disappeared and new beings have arrived from outer space, how will we be able to signal to them that they mustn't use or even walk on the land in question? The government agency gave linguist and anthropologist Tom Sebeok the job of creating a form of communication that could overcome these difficulties. Having examined all possible solutions, Sebeok concluded that there was no language, even pictorial, that was likely to be comprehensible outside the context that had given rise to it. We are unable to interpret the prehistoric figures we find in caves with any certainty. Even ideographic language may not be properly understood. According to him, the only possible solution would be to create religious brotherhoods and have them circulate a taboo like 'Don't touch such-and-such' or 'Don't eat so-and-so'. A taboo can be maintained over generations. I had another idea, but NASA weren't paying me so I kept it to myself. It was to bury the nuclear waste in such a way that the first layer was very dilute and therefore not too radioactive, the second a little more radioactive, and so on. If this being accidentally stuck his hand – or whatever he used for a hand – into the waste, he would only lose a finger. But then, we can't be sure that he would not have persisted.

J.-C. C. | When we discovered the first Assyrian libraries, we didn't have the faintest clue about cuneiform writing. Again, questions of loss and longevity. What to save?

What to pass down, and how? How to be sure that the language I use today will be understood tomorrow and beyond tomorrow? A civilisation isn't a civilisation unless it asks itself these questions. You talk of a time when all the linguistic codes have vanished, and languages are mute or incomprehensible. One can also imagine the opposite: I might paint senseless graffiti on a wall today, only for someone in the future to claim that they have deciphered it. For a year or so, I tried inventing new types of script; no doubt in times to come, people would be able to attribute some sense to them.

U.E. | Of course they would – there's nothing like nonsense to provoke interpretation.

J.-C. C. | Or interpretation to generate nonsense. Which is the great gift of the Surrealists, who bring together utterly unrelated words in order to draw out a hidden meaning.

U. E. | The same goes for philosophy. Bertrand Russell's work hasn't provoked nearly as much interpretation as Heidegger's. Why is that? Because Russell is particularly clear and easy to understand, whereas Heidegger is obscure. I'm not saying that one was right and the other wrong. Personally, I'm suspicious of both of them. But when Russell says something stupid he says

177

it clearly, whereas with Heidegger even a truism is hard to spot. So if you want to go down in history, you'd better be obscure. Even Heraclitus knew that . . .

But let me digress for a moment: do you know why the Presocratics only wrote fragments?

J.-C. C. | No.

U. E. | Because they lived in ruins. Joking aside, our only knowledge of these fragments is often through the comments they've provoked, sometimes centuries later. We owe almost everything we know of Stoic philosophy – an intellectual achievement whose full importance we are probably not yet aware of – to Sextus Empiricus' critiques. In the same way, we know of several Presocratic fragments only through the writings of Aëtius, who, as you can tell from his work, was a complete fool. We have to wonder whether what he wrote was even true to Presocratic philosophy. There's also the case of the Gauls as reported by Caesar, and the Germans according to Tacitus. We know something of these peoples only through the reports of their enemies.

J.-C. C. | You could say that about the heretics denounced by the Church Fathers.

U. E. | It's rather as if our knowledge of twentieth-century philosophy came from Ratzinger's encyclicals.

J.-C. C. | I've always been fascinated by Simon Magus, and once wrote a book about him. He was a contemporary of Christ who is only known through the Acts of the Apostles, which is to say according to those who denounced him as a heretic and accused him of what they named 'simony', the sin of buying magic powers, in this case those of Jesus from St Peter. And that's almost the only thing we know about him. But who was he really? He had disciples, and people said he could perform miracles. He can't have been the absurd quack his enemies portrayed.

U. E. | We know from the enemies of the Paulicians and the Bogomils that they ate children. But then people said the same thing of the Jews. Every enemy of everything has always eaten children.

J.-C. C. | A large part of what we know of the past, which has usually come to us in books, is therefore the work of halfwits, fools or people with a grudge. It's rather as if all traces of the past had disappeared, and our only tools to reconstruct them were the works of literary madmen.

U. E. | A character in my *Foucault's Pendulum* wonders whether you couldn't say the same thing about the Evangelists. Maybe what Jesus said was completely different from what they reported.

J.-C. C. | It's very likely that he did say something different. We often forget that our most ancient Christian texts are the Epistles of St Paul. The Gospels come later. Paul, who was therefore the real inventor of Christianity, was a very complex man. It seems that he had some rather lively exchanges with Jesus' brother James regarding the then-crucial subject of circumcision. After all, Jesus continued to go to synagogue, as did his brother after Jesus' death. They remained Jewish. It was Paul who separated Christianity from Judaism and preached to the 'Gentiles', meaning the non-Jews. He was the founding father.

U. E. | Paul was an extremely bright man, and soon realised that in order for Jesus' words to have the greatest possible impact, he had to sell Christianity to the Romans. That's why, in the tradition that starts with Paul and therefore the Gospels, Pilate is a coward, certainly, but not truly guilty. So it was really the Jews who were responsible for the death of Jesus.

J.-C. C. | Paul doubtless also realised that he would never be able to sell Jesus to the Jews as a new God, the only

God, because at the time Judaism was still a strong new religion, conquering even, proselytising, whereas the Greco-Roman religion was in rapid decline. This wasn't the case with Roman civilisation itself, though, which methodically transformed the classical world, unifying it and imposing on its peoples the centuries-long *Pax Romana*. Bush's swaggering America was never universally legitimate enough or sufficiently well defined to offer the world that kind of peace.

U. E. | If we're talking about madmen we should definitely mention the American televangelists. A quick flick through the American TV channels on a Sunday morning will give you an idea of the extent and seriousness of the problem. What Sacha Baron Cohen depicts in *Borat* is definitely not the fruits of his imagination. I remember that if you wanted to teach at the Oral Roberts University in Oklahoma during the Sixties (Oral Roberts was one of those Sunday televangelists), you had to answer questions like 'Do you speak in tongues?', which implies an ability to speak in a language that no one knows but everyone understands, as in The Acts of the Apostles. A colleague of mine was accepted because he replied, 'Not yet.'

J.-C. C. | I've actually been to several services in the States, complete with laying-on of hands, fake healing and artificial ecstasy. It was scary. At times I felt like I was in a mental hospital. But at the same time I don't think it's worth worrying about these things too much. I always think that if God were to exist and suddenly take the side of these raging zealots, then religious fundamentalism and fanaticism would be very serious indeed. But one can't really say that He has committed himself to one side or the other, not so far at least. It seems to me that these movements spring up, but then lose momentum, having never – of course – had access to divine intervention, and having been worthless from the outset. The danger is perhaps more that the American neo-creationists will end up winning the right for biblical 'truths' to be taught in schools in place of science, which would definitely be a backward step. They are not the only ones trying to impose their views in this way. I once visited a rabbinical school in Paris' rue des Rosiers where 'teachers' were teaching that the world was created by God a little more than 6,000 years ago, and that Satan had arranged the prehistoric remains into sedimentary layers in order to trick us.

That was about fifteen years ago. I can't imagine things have changed much. These 'teachings' can be considered akin to St Paul's attack on Greek science. Faith is always stronger than knowledge – it may surprise us, we may not like it, but that's how it is.

And yet it would be an exaggeration to suggest that these pernicious teachings have had a drastic effect on the general development of things. No, things are what they are. It's also worth remembering that Voltaire was taught by Jesuits.

U. E. | Every great atheist had a religious education.

J.-C. C. | And much as religion tried to silence it, Greek science triumphed in the end. Despite the path of truth being littered with obstacles, funeral pyres, prisons and the odd death camp.

U. E. | The rebirth of religion does not happen in times of political conservatism. Quite the opposite. It flourishes in hyper-technological times such as our own, in periods of major moral decline, when great ideologies are on their last legs. It's then that we need to believe in something. It was when the Roman Empire was at the height of its powers, when its senators were frolicking openly with prostitutes and wearing lipstick, that Christianity took root. It's a matter of natural rebalancing.

These days, there are several expressions of this need to believe. For example, an interest in the science of the tarot, or in New Age thinking. Or the return of anti-Darwinism, on the part of not only fundamentalist

Protestants, but also right-wing Catholics (as in Italy at the moment). It's been a long time since the Catholic Church was particularly bothered about the theory of evolution: we have known since the early Church Fathers that the Bible teaches through metaphor and that therefore the six days of Creation could perfectly well refer to six geological eras. And in any case Genesis is very Darwinian. Man only comes into being after the other animals, and he is created out of dust. He is therefore both a product of the earth and the pinnacle of evolution.

The only thing the faithful would insist upon is that the evolution was not random, but the result of 'intelligent design'. And yet the current controversy is not about design, but about the whole of Darwinism. This is clearly a step backwards. Once again we are turning to mythology as a refuge from the threats of technology. To the extent that we're even seeing collective veneration of a figure like Padre Pio.

J.-C. C. | But I'd like to put a different slant on this. We seem to be blaming everything on faith. But there were more than 100 million violent deaths on our planet between 1933, when Hitler came to power, and Stalin's death twenty years later. More, perhaps, than in any other war throughout history. And both Marxism and Nazism were savagely atheist. When

184

the world woke up dumbfounded after the massacre, it seemed absolutely natural to return to religious practices.

U. E. | But the Nazis used to shout '*Gott mit uns*' ('God is with us'), and were full of pagan religiosity. Once atheism becomes a state religion, as in the Soviet Union, there is no longer any difference between a believer and an atheist. Either of them might become fundamentalists, extremists. I once wrote that it isn't true that religion is the opiate of the masses, as Marx claimed. Opium would have neutralised the masses, anaesthetised them, put them to sleep. Actually, religion stirs up the crowds: it is the cocaine of the masses.

J.-C. C. | Or perhaps a mixture of opium and cocaine. It's certainly true that today's Islamic fundamentalism seems to be taking up the torch from militant atheism, and that we can now look back on Marxism and Nazism as two strange pagan religions. But what massacres!

Nothing can put an end to vanity

J.-P. DE T. | By the time it reaches us, the past has been severely distorted, especially when its transmission has been compromised by human stupidity. You have suggested that culture prefers to retain nothing but the peaks of creation, the Himalayas, and to leave behind much of what is not to our credit. Could you give some examples of this latter category of 'masterpiece'?

J.-C. C. | Your question makes me think of an incredible three-volume work called *La Folie de Jésus* in which the author, Charles Binet-Sanglé, argues that Jesus was in fact 'physically and mentally defective'. Interestingly, Binet-Sanglé was a highly respected professor of medicine, and the work was published in 1908, at the beginning of the twentieth century. Let me quote a few gems: 'Having presented with long-term anorexia and an attack of hematidrosis, he died prematurely on the cross, losing consciousness from an inability to breathe brought on by the existence of a pleural effusion in all likelihood tuberculosis-related and on the left side . . .' The author specifies that Jesus was short and thin, despite coming from a family of wine-growers who drank good wine and lived well. In short, 'for the last one thousand nine hundred years, Western civilisation has been built around a faulty diagnosis'. This is a crazy book, but written so seriously that it commands respect.

I own another gem of a book, by a nineteenth-century French prelate who had the revelation that atheists were not depraved, or bad people; they were merely insane. The cure was therefore very simple. They must be kept in atheist asylums and treated; this treatment should consist of cold showers and the mandatory daily reading of twenty pages from the works of Louis XIV's court preacher Jacques-Bénigne Bossuet. In this way, most of them would be restored to sanity. The obviously unhinged author, who was called Lefebre, took his book to the great psychiatrists of the day, Pinel and Esquirol, who of course refused to see him. By the way, my TV film *Credo* (directed twenty-five years ago by Jacques Deray) portrayed the polar opposite of a wild prelate determined to lock up atheists and subject them to cold showers. I'd read a paragraph in *Le Monde* about a history professor in Kiev, Ukraine, who had been arrested by the KGB, interrogated, convicted of insanity and incarcerated, all because he believed in God. The film was an imaginative portrayal of the entire cross-examination.

U. E. | Let's go much further back in time. When I was working on my book about the search for the perfect language I came across some crazy linguists, inventors of wild theories about the roots of language. The most entertaining were the nationalists, who were totally convinced that their country's language was the language of Adam. According to Guillaume Postel, the Celts were descendants of Noah; in Spain, linguists argued that Castilian went right back to Tubal, son of Japheth. Goropius Becanus was convinced that every language stemmed from one primary language, the dialect of Antwerp. Abraham Mylius, on the other hand, showed how Hebrew had given rise to the Teutonic language, the purest form of the Antwerp dialect. The Baron de Ryckholt insisted that Flemish was the only language spoken in the cradle of humanity. Also in the seventeenth century, Georg Stiernhielm claimed in his *De linguarum origine praefatio* that Gothic – which for him was ancient Norwegian – was the first among all known languages. A Swedish scholar, Olaus Rudbeck, argued in his (3,000-page-long) *Atlantica sive Mannheim vera Japheti posterorum sedes ac patria* that Sweden was Japheth's homeland, and Swedish Adam's original language. One of Rudbeck's contemporaries, Andreas Kempe, wrote a parody of all these theories in which God speaks Swedish, Adam speaks Danish, and Eve is seduced by a French-speaking serpent. Later there was Antoine de Rivarol, who claimed not that French was the original language, but that it was the most rational – English being too complicated, German too brutal, Italian too confused, etc.

After this we come to Heidegger, who asserted that philosophy could only be undertaken in Greek or German – so tough luck for Locke and Descartes. Then there were the pyramidologists, the most famous of whom, the Scottish astronomer Charles Piazzi Smyth, found all the dimensions of the universe in the Giza pyramid. It's still an extremely active field, which these days operates predominantly online. Just type 'pyramid' into a search engine. Apparently the height of the pyramid multiplied by one million represents the distance between the Earth and the Sun; its weight multiplied by a billion is the weight of the Earth; if you double the length of its four sides you'll get one-sixtieth of a degree of the latitude of the equator: the Giza pyramid is therefore built to a scale of 1:43,200 of the Earth.

J.-C.C. | It's a bit like those people who agonise over whether President Mitterrand was the reincarnation of Thutmose II.

J.-P. DE T. | Then there's the glass pyramid at the Louvre,

which people insist contains 666 panes of glass, despite the repeated denial by both the design team and the builders. But then Dan Brown has confirmed it . . .

U. E. | Our catalogue of lunacy could go on for ever. For example, you probably know of the infamous Dr Tissot and his research on masturbation as a cause of blindness, deafness, dementia praecox and other misfortunes. And then there's another author, whose name I forget, who argued that syphilis is a dangerous disease because it can lead to tuberculosis.

A certain Mr Andrieu, in 1869, published a book on the dangers of toothpicks. A Mr Ecochoard wrote about different methods of impalement, and in 1858 a Mr Foumel held forth about the value of being beaten with a stick, providing a list of famous artists and writers who had benefited from this practice, from Boileau to Voltaire to Mozart.

J.-C. C. | We mustn't forget Edgar Bérillon, member of the Institut de France, who in 1915 wrote that the Germans defecated more than the French. According to him, you could establish which of them had travelled through a particular place from the quantity of excrement left behind. A traveller could thus ascertain that he had crossed the border from Lorraine to Rhineland-Palatinate by checking out the size of the turds at the side of the road. Bérillon speaks of the 'increased peristaltic movement' of the German race.

U. E. | In 1843 a certain Chesnier-Duchen created a system to translate French into hieroglyphics, which would allow it to be understood the world over. While in 1779 the noble Mr Chassaignon wrote a four-volume work entitled *Cataractes de l'imagination: déluge de la scribomanie, vomissement littéraire, hémorragie encyclopédique, monstre des monstres**, whose content I shall leave to your imagination (it includes a tribute to the tribute, and a meditation on the roots of liquorice).

A most interesting phenomenon is madmen who write about madmen. In *Les Fous littéraires*, Gustave Brunet does not distinguish between crazy books and serious books written by people who probably suffered from psychiatric problems. His delightful list of literary madmen includes Cyrano de Bergerac, Sade, Fourier, Newton, Poe and Whitman, but also Henrion, who in 1718 published an essay on Adam's vital statistics. Brunet recognises that Socrates cannot be described as a writer, having never written, but argues that a man who claimed to have his own familiar or spirit (a clear

---

* The title translates roughly as *Torrents of Imagination: A Deluge of Writing-Mania, Literary Vomiting, Encyclopaedic Haemorrhage and Monster of Monsters.*

194

sign of monomania) should certainly be classified as mad.

In another book on literary madmen, André Blavier lists 1,500 works, whose authors include advocates of new cosmogonies, hygienists who recommend walking backwards, a certain Madrolle who explored the theology of the railway, a man called Passon who, in his 1829 work *Démonstration de l'immobilité de la Terre,* argued that the Earth doesn't move, and a Tardy who argued in 1878 that the Earth turns on its own axis every forty-eight hours.

J.-P. DE T. | *Foucault's Pendulum* features what in English is called a vanity press, namely a publishing house where authors pay for their own books to be published. These too have launched a few 'masterpieces'. . .

U. E. | Yes. And I wasn't making it up. Before writing the novel I had written an exposé of that kind of publishing. You send your text to one of these companies. They praise its great literary merit and offer to publish. You are thrilled. They give you a contract to sign, which states that you must finance the publication of your manuscript, and that in return the editors will do their best to obtain lots of good press and even – imagine – some flattering blurbs. The contract doesn't specify how many copies will be printed, but emphasises that unsold copies will be destroyed 'unless you announce your intention to purchase'. The publisher then prints 300 copies – 100 for the author who sends them to friends and family, and 200 for the newspapers, who throw them straight in the bin.

J.-C. C. | As soon as they see the publisher's name.

U. E. | However, the company also publishes low-circulation magazines, which soon feature reviews praising this 'important' book. To impress his friends and family, the author buys, say, 100 more copies, which are speedily printed off by the publisher. A year later, the author is told that sales were not very good and that the rest of the print run (which he is told was 10,000 copies) will have to be destroyed. How many would he like to purchase? The author is horribly distressed at the prospective destruction of his precious book and buys 3,000. The publisher quickly prints 3,000 copies that didn't previously exist and sells them to the author. The publisher has no distribution costs at all, so it's an extremely profitable business.

Another example of vanity publishing (and there are many, many more that I could mention) is a book that I do in fact possess, the *Dizionario biografico degli italiani* – a biographical dictionary of contemporary

Italians. The idea is that one pays to feature in it. So it might list 'Pavese Cesare, born 9 September 1908 at Santo Stefano Belbo, died Turin, 26 August 1950' with the note 'author and translator'. And that's it. Followed by two whole pages on a Paolizzi Deodato whom no one has ever heard of. Perhaps the greatest of these unknown celebrities is a certain Giulio Ser Giacomi, who published his correspondence with Einstein and Pius XII in a huge 1,500-page tome; the book, however, contains only the letters he wrote to both men, because of course neither of them ever replied.

J.-C. C. | I did once pay to have a book produced, but with no intention of selling it. It was about the actor Jean Carmet. I wrote it after his death, for some of his friends and family, and a colleague helped me type it up on my computer. We then printed fifty copies, with a paperback cover. Anyone can 'do' a book these days. Distributing it is another matter entirely.

U. E. | One of the heavyweight Italian newspapers will put out any reader's book for a very modest sum. The publishers don't put their name on the book, as they don't wish to answer for the author's ideas. I imagine that this kind of business will decrease the vanity-press industry, but probably increase the trade in publishing by the vain. Nothing can put an end to vanity.

But all this has a positive side, too. These publications are anonymous, in the same way that the unpublished texts circulating freely on the Internet are the modern version of samizdat, which was the only way to disseminate ideas under a dictatorship and thus escape censorship. Those who used to produce samizdat books at great personal cost can now put their texts online in relative safety.

The practice of samizdat goes back a long way. There are seventeenth-century books published in obviously invented cities called things like Francopolis. These were books which could have had the authors accused of heresy, so the authors and printers created secret objects. If you own a book from that time without a publisher's name on the title page, it is definitively a clandestine publication. There were lots of them. The best thing you could hope for, if you disagreed with the party line under the Stalinist dictatorship, was to produce a samizdat work. Your text would be distributed through a secret network.

J.-C. C. | In Poland between 1981 and 1984, anonymous hands used to slip samizdat texts under people's doors at night.

U. E. | In democracies, in which censorship isn't supposed to exist, the electronic equivalent of this practice is the text declined by every publishing house and then posted online by the author. I know young Italian writers who have taken that route. It's worked out very well for some of them – an editor has read their work online and made contact.

J.-P. DE T. | We might seem as if we're placing all our faith in the faultless good taste and intuition of the publishing houses. But we know that it's far from infallible. Perhaps we should also discuss this interesting and entertaining aspect of book history. Are editors really better able to see into the future than their authors?

U. E. | They have shown that they can sometimes be stupid enough to reject a masterpiece. That's another chapter in the history of idiocy. The first reader's report on Proust's *In Search of Lost Time* said: 'It may be a lack of intelligence on my part, but I fail to understand why it should take thirty pages to describe how someone tosses and turns in their bed, unable to sleep.' About *Moby-Dick*: 'There is little chance that a book such as this would interest a young readership.' To Flaubert, about *Madame Bovary*: 'Sir, you have buried your novel beneath a hotchpotch of detail that is very well done, but utterly superfluous.' To Emily

Dickinson: 'Your rhymes don't work.' To Colette, about *Claudine at School*: 'I fear that this would sell no more than ten copies.' To George Orwell about *Animal Farm*: 'It's no good trying to sell the Americans a novel about animals.' About Anne Frank's *Diary*: 'This kid doesn't seem to have the faintest idea that her book is no more than an object of curiosity.' But it isn't only publishers – what about Hollywood producers? Here's a talent scout in 1928 describing Fred Astaire's first performance: 'He can't act, he can't sing, he's bald and he can dance a little.' And about Clark Gable: 'What are we supposed to do with someone with ears like that?'

J.-C.C. | That's quite a list. Let's try and imagine the percentage of books, out of everything that has ever been written and published around the world, that can be said to be beautiful, moving, unforgettable . . . or even just worth reading. One per cent? One out of every thousand? Our attitude towards books is reverential, even sacred. But actually, if you look carefully, a horrific proportion of our libraries is made up of books written by the utterly talentless, or by halfwits and crazy people. The great majority of the 300,000 scrolls kept in the Library of Alexandria are bound to have been complete rubbish.

U.E. | I don't think Alexandria contained that many books. As we've said, we always overestimate when talking about the ancient libraries. They've proven that the most famous libraries of the Middle Ages contained at the most 400 books! There must of course have been more at Alexandria, because they say that 40,000 scrolls burned in the first fire, in Caesar's time, and that the fire only affected one wing. But we must be careful not to compare our libraries with those of ancient times. The production of papyrus cannot be compared to the production of printed books. It takes a great deal longer to create a unique, handwritten scroll or codex than to print a huge number of copies of a single book.

J.-C. C. | But the Library of Alexandria was an extremely ambitious project, a state library that absolutely cannot be compared to the private library of a king, even a great king, or the library of a monastery. Alexandria is better compared to the Library of Pergamum, which also burned down. Perhaps every library is fated to burn down eventually.

J.-P. DE T. | But we now know that fire doesn't only destroy great works of literature.

J.-C. C. | Yes, we think we know that now. The majority of the lost books would certainly have been rather mediocre, but some of them would still have been entertaining, and even in a way educational. Those kinds of books have always given people a lot of pleasure. Others disturb us, when we stop to think about the mental health of the author. Then there are the bad books – aggressive, hateful, injurious books inciting war and crime. Terrifying books. Instruments of death. If we were publishers, would we have published *Mein Kampf*?

U.E. | In certain countries, there are laws against revisionism. But there is a difference between the right not to publish a book and the right to destroy it once it has been published.

J.-C. C. | Céline's widow, for example, has always blocked the republication of *Trifles for a Massacre*. I remember a time when you couldn't get hold of it for love or money.

U.E. | I wanted to use an extract from *Trifles* about the ugliness of the Jew from the anti-Semite's perspective in my book *On Ugliness*, but the author's widow refused to grant my editor reproduction rights. Not that you can't find the entire text on the Internet – on a Nazi site, of course.

I've mentioned the madmen who insist that their national language was the first and original language.

But here's someone else who made claims that were part reasonable, part nonsense. I'm thinking of the seventeenth-century French Protestant Isaac de La Peyrère's book *Prae-Adamitae*. It explains that the world is much older than the 6,000 years claimed in the Bible because Chinese ancestry can be traced back much further. Christ's mission to redeem humanity from original sin was therefore only of interest to the Mediterranean Jewish world, and not these other worlds, which had not been affected by original sin. Which is a bit what the libertines were saying about the plurality of worlds: if the many-world theory is correct, how to explain that Jesus Christ came to Earth rather than anywhere else? Unless one thinks he was crucified on many planets . . .

J.-C. C. | When Buñuel and I were working on *The Milky Way* – which explores the heresies of the Christian religion – I dreamed up a scene we both loved, but that would have been too expensive to shoot and so doesn't feature in the film. A flying saucer lands with great fanfare. The cover or cockpit opens and an antennaed green creature emerges, brandishing a cross upon which another antennaed green creature is nailed.

But coming back down to Earth, let me mention the Spanish conquistadors. When they landed in the Americas they couldn't understand how people had never heard of the Christian God, or of Jesus our Saviour. Hadn't Christ said: 'Go ye therefore, and teach all nations'?

God couldn't have made a mistake in asking his disciples to preach the new truth to all men. The logical conclusion, therefore, was that these beings were not men. As Sepúlveda said, 'God didn't want them in his kingdom.' In order to prove the humanity of the American Indians, some went so far as to invent the discovery of crosses, presenting them as confirmation of the presence of Christian apostles on the continent before the arrival of the Spanish. Unfortunately, the sleight of hand was discovered.

In praise of stupidity

J.-P. DE T. | If I'm not mistaken, both of you are great lovers of human stupidity . . .

J.-C. C. | Faithful lovers, yes. Human stupidity can count on us. The impetus for my getting together with Guy Bechtel in the Sixties to start work on our dictionary of stupidity (*Dictionnaire de la bêtise* – since reprinted several times) was the thought: 'Why study only the history of brilliance, why only masterpieces and the great milestones of the mind?' Human stupidity, so beloved of Flaubert, seemed to us far more widespread – obviously – but also more fertile, more revealing and in a certain sense more accurate. We wrote an introduction called 'In praise of stupidity'. We even offered to give classes.

The nonsense written about Blacks, Jews, Chinese people, women, great artists, etc. seemed to us far more revealing than the intelligent analyses. During the Restoration, the ultra-conservative Archbishop de Quélen declared from the pulpit of Notre-Dame to an audience of French aristocrats newly returned from abroad, 'Not only was Jesus Christ the son of God, he was of excellent stock on his mother's side.' This says a great deal, not only about the archbishop (of incidental interest), but also about the mentality and culture of the time.

It also reminds me of the notorious anti-Semite Houston Stewart Chamberlain's classic remark: 'Whoever maintains that Jesus Christ was a Jew is either ignorant or dishonest.'

U. E. | I would, however, like us to create some definitions – especially important with the subject at hand! In one of my books I distinguished between the fool, the idiot and the person with a very low IQ (let's call him a simpleton). The simpleton – who aims his spoon at his forehead instead of his mouth, and doesn't understand what he is told – is of no interest here; his case is well understood. Foolishness, on the other hand, is a social quality, but it is important to define it clearly because for some people 'idiot' and 'fool' mean the same thing. The fool is a person who says something he shouldn't at a given moment, who is always putting his foot in it. The idiot is different – it's not that he's socially inept, but that his logic is faulty. Initially he seems to reason well enough, and you can't quite work out what's wrong. And that's why he's dangerous.

I'd better give an example. The idiot might say: 'Everyone who lived in Piraeus was an Athenian. All Athenians were Greek. Therefore, all Greeks lived in Piraeus.' You suspect something isn't right, because you know that some Greeks lived in Sparta, for example.

But you can't find a way to prove how and where he went wrong. You'd have to know the rules of formal logic to do that.

J.-C.C. | For me, the idiot isn't content with just being wrong. He has to broadcast his error for all to hear. Idiocy is unbelievably strident. 'We now know for sure that . . .' followed by some utter rubbish.

U. E. | You're quite right. Any banal, commonplace truth becomes an idiocy when it's shouted all over the place.

J.-C.C. | Flaubert says that stupidity is wanting to draw conclusions, to come to absolute and definitive answers, closing the issue once and for all. But this stupidity, often taken as the truth by some sections of society, can be extremely helpful to those of us looking at history with the benefit of hindsight. As we have said, the history of beauty and intelligence, on which education concentrates – or, rather, on which others have decided education should concentrate – is only a tiny part of human activity. Perhaps one should even consider compiling, as in fact you are doing, a general history of mistakes and absurdities, as well as of ugliness.

U. E. | We've talked about Aëtius and the way he described the work of the Presocratics. There's no doubt about it, the guy was an idiot. It also occurs to me, given what you've said, that stupidity isn't exactly the same thing as idiocy. It's more like a way of acting it out.

J.-C. C. | In an emphatic, often bombastic kind of way.

U. E. | You can be an idiot without being totally stupid. An accidental idiot.

J.-C. C. | Yes, but in that case you don't make a profession of it.

U. E. | It's true that one can make a living from stupidity. In your example, it seems to me that saying Jesus was 'of excellent stock' is not entirely idiotic. Simply because, from an explanatory point of view, it is true. It is, I think, more a case of foolishness: I can say that someone is of good stock, but I can't say it about Jesus because it is obviously less important than him being the Son of God. So Quélen was stating a historical fact, but an irrelevant one. The fool tends to speak without due consideration.

J.-C. C. | I'm thinking of that phrase: 'I'm not well bred. But my children are.' Unless ironic, this is the statement of a complacent fool. But let's come back to His Grace de Quélen, who was after all the Archbishop of Paris

– very conservative-minded, certainly, but with tremendous moral authority over the France of the time.

U. E. | We had better refine our definition, then. Stupidity is a way of acting out one's idiocy with persistence and pride.

J.-C. C. | Not bad. We could also enrich this discussion with quotations from those – and they are many – who have sought to destroy what we today consider our greatest authors and artists. It's important to remember that insults always speak louder than praise. And true poets tread their paths through a storm of insults. Beethoven's Fifth was called a 'vulgar din' and 'the end of music'. There's an astonishing list of illustrious names implicated in the garlands of insults hung around the necks of Shakespeare, Balzac, Hugo, and so on. Flaubert himself said about Balzac: 'What a man he would have been, if only he'd known how to write.'

And then there is patriotic, military, nationalistic and racist stupidity. The entry on Jews in my dictionary of stupidity is full of quotes that are less hateful than simply stupid. Nastily stupid. For example: Jews have an innate taste for money. Proof: when a Jewish mother is having a difficult labour, all you have to do is shake some coins near the belly and the baby Jew will emerge with his hands held out. That was written in 1888, by a certain Fernand Grégoire. Written and published. Then there's Fourier, claiming that Jews are the 'the plague and cholera of the social body'. Proudhon himself wrote in his journal: 'This race must be sent back to Asia, or exterminated.' These are 'truths' put forward by people who often called themselves scientists. 'Truths' to chill your bones.

U. E. | So is that idiocy, or simple-mindedness? Joyce gives us the ultimate foolishness (in my understanding of the word) in this piece of dialogue: 'I heard your brother was dead,' says Skeffington. The response: 'And he was only ten years old.' Skeffington's next comment: 'Well, that's still painful.'

J.-C. C. | Stupidity is often close to error. Your research on fakes and falsities has always interested me because I'm so keen on stupidity. The education system studiously ignores both. Every age has its truths on the one hand and its notorious (and great) follies on the other, but the education system only cares to teach and transmit the truths. One could say that stupidity is filtered out. We have 'intelligence correctness' as well as 'political correctness'. In other words, there's a right way to think. Whether we like it or not.

U. E. | The litmus test allows us to find out whether something is acid or alkaline. Our litmus test should likewise allow us to establish whether we are dealing with an idiot or a fool. But to return to your linking of stupidity and the false – being wrong is not always the result of idiocy or folly. It can be a simple error. Ptolemy believed in good faith that the Earth did not move. He made a mistake, as a result of faulty scientific data. But we may discover tomorrow that the Earth actually doesn't orbit the Sun, and praise Ptolemy's wisdom.

Acting in bad faith is saying the opposite of what one believes to be true. But people are always making mistakes in good faith. Error, therefore, is present throughout human history, and that's a good thing, because otherwise we would be gods. The notion of 'falsehood' that I've studied is actually very subtle. There is the fake imitation of something called 'original', which must be totally identical to its model. In this case there is an indiscernibility, in Leibniz's sense of the word, between the original and the fake. The error here is to attribute the value of truth to something one knows is a fake. Then there is the false reasoning of Ptolemy, who was wrong in good faith. But he wasn't attempting to state that the Earth doesn't move when he actually knew that it orbited the Sun. No. Ptolemy really thought that the Earth didn't move. Falsification is completely different from what hindsight shows us, in Ptolemy's case, was simply an erroneous understanding.

J.-C. C. | Picasso used to say, with a precision that isn't going to make our efforts at definition any easier, that he too could create fake Picassos. He even boasted that he'd painted the best fake Picassos in the world.

U. E. | De Chirico also confessed to painting fake Chiricos. And I have to admit that I myself have produced a fake Eco. An Italian satirical magazine rather like *Private Eye* was producing a special edition of the Italian broadsheet *Il Corriere della Sera* devoted to aliens who were landing on Earth. A fake, of course. They asked me for a fake article, a kind of Eco parody.

J.-C. C. | It's a way of escaping oneself – one's flesh, one's material being. Maybe one's mind, too.

U. E. | But also of critiquing oneself, bringing out one's clichés, for it is those clichés that I have to repeat in order to 'do an Eco'. Producing a fake of oneself is a very healthy challenge.

J.-C. C. | The same goes for that study of stupidity, which took us several years to write. During those years, Bechtel and I only read very bad books, and a lot of

214

them. We would pore over library catalogues and get an idea of the treasures awaiting us from some of the titles. We knew we'd struck gold when we came across a title like *Of the Influence of the Velocipede on Good Manners.*

U. E. | But it does become a problem when these people make their way into your life. As I've said, I once wrote about the madmen published by vanity presses, summarising their ideas with what I thought was obvious irony. But some of them didn't notice the irony and wrote to thank me for taking their ideas seriously. The same goes for *Foucault's Pendulum*, which lays into the 'bearers of truth', and yet resulted in unexpected praise and enthusiasm from them. I (or rather my wife and secretary, who screen them) still receive calls from a certain Grand Master Templar.

J.-C. C. | We published a letter in our dictionary of stupidity that I think you'll find amusing. We came across it in a magazine for Apostolic Missions (yes, we read even that). A priest is thanking his correspondent for sending a miracle water, which 'had a very positive impact on the sick man but without him knowing it'. The priest continues: 'I had this man – who for four years had been hovering between life and death, a man who, likewise for four years, had resisted me with desperate stubbornness and horrifying blasphemy – unwittingly drink the water for nine days, and after this novena he expired peacefully, speaking words of mercy that were all the more comforting for being so unexpected.'

U. E. | The difficulty in deciding whether this man is a simpleton, an idiot or a fool stems from the fact that these are ideal types, or *Idealtypen* as the Germans would say. Most of the time, one individual will exhibit a mixture of all three. The reality is much more complex than the typology.

J.-C. C. | It's been years since I've thought seriously about all of this, and I'm struck again by the value of studying stupidity. Not only does it challenge the sanctification of the book, it also reminds us that we're all constantly in danger of spouting similar nonsense. We're never far from saying something idiotic – as we can see from this comment by Chateaubriand, of all people, talking about Napoleon, whom he didn't much like: 'He is a great winner of battles, certainly, but apart from that, any old general is more capable.'

J.-P. DE T. | Could you expand a little on this shared passion of yours for these reminders of humanity's limits and imperfections? Would you say it was a covert kind of compassion?

J.-C. C. | I had a sudden revelation when I was about thirty and had finished my higher education and read most of the classic texts. I had fought in the Algerian war from 1959 to 1960, and I suddenly realised the total uselessness and even futility of what I had been taught. I started reading texts on colonisation that were more idiotic, and violent, than I'd ever thought possible, and that nobody had ever encouraged me to read. I started to think that I might be better off abandoning the well-trodden path and checking out the surroundings, the wilderness, the bush, the swamps even. Guy Bechtel's experiences had been similar, and then we met in the preparation classes for the École Normale Supérieure.

U. E. | I think we're on the same wavelength, even if we're coming from slightly different places. When you asked me to write a conclusion, Jean-Philippe, for your encyclopaedia of death and immortality,* I suggested that in order to accept the notion of one's own death, one

* *La Mort et l'Immortalité, Encyclopédie des savoirs et des croyances*, compiled by Frédéric Lenoir and Jean-Philippe de Tonnac, Bayard, 2004 – not yet translated into English.

has to convince oneself that everyone who will survive is a cretin, so there's no point spending any more time with them. Which is a funny way of saying something true – namely, that we spend our lives cultivating the great human virtues. And the human being is a truly remarkable creature. He has discovered fire, built cities, written magnificent poems, interpreted the world, invented mythologies, etc. But at the same time he has never ceased waging war on his fellow humans, being totally wrong, destroying his environment, etc. This mixture of great intellectual powers and base idiocy creates an approximately neutral outcome. So when we decide to explore human stupidity, we are somehow paying tribute to this creature who is part genius, part fool. And once you start approaching death, as we both are, you start thinking that the idiocy has the edge – which is clearly the ultimate consolation. Let's say a plumber comes to my house to repair a leak in the bathroom, takes a big chunk of my money and leaves, only for us to find that the bath is still leaking. I will cheer myself up by saying to my wife: 'The guy's a simpleton. Otherwise would he be repairing baths badly? No. He'd be teaching semiotics at the University of Bologna.'

J.-C. C. | The first thing you learn when studying human stupidity is that you're a fool. Obviously. You can't blithely call others fools without realising that their stupidity is a mirror. A permanent, accurate, loyal mirror.

U. E. | Let's not fall prey to Epimenides' paradox. Epimenides said that all Cretans are liars. He is Cretan, so he must be a liar. If some cretin tells you that everyone else is a cretin, the fact of being a cretin doesn't mean that he might not be telling the truth. If he then adds that all others are cretins 'like him', he is positively intelligent. And therefore not a cretin. Because others spend their lives trying to make you forget that's what they are.

There's also the risk of falling prey to another paradox, described by Owen. Everyone is a cretin, except you and me. And actually, deep down, when I think about it, you . . .

J.-C. C. | The human mind is amazing. The books that you and I collect bear witness to the truly dizzying aspects of our imagination. And it's particularly hard to differentiate between rambling craziness on the one hand and stupidity on the other.

U. E. | I've just thought of another example of idiocy. It's about Neuhaus, the author of a tract on the Rosicrucian Order written in 1623, when the French were wondering whether or not the order had actually existed. 'The mere fact that they hid the fact of their existence is in itself proof that they existed,' says Neuhaus. The proof that they existed is that they denied existing.

J.-C. C. | That seems quite sound to me.

J.-P. DE T. | Perhaps – and this is just an idea – we can see human stupidity as an ancient scourge that our new, universally accessible technologies will help wipe out? Would you subscribe to this positive interpretation?

J.-C. C. | I refuse to be pessimistic about our age. Pessimism is too easy, and it's ubiquitous. And yet . . . perhaps I'll quote Michel Serres' reply to a journalist who was asking him – I can't remember why – about the decision to build the Aswan Dam. The committee was made up of hydraulic engineers, specialists on different materials, developers and maybe even some ecologists, but no philosophers, and no Egyptologists. Michel Serres was shocked. And the journalist was shocked that he was shocked, and asked, 'What would be the point of having a philosopher on a committee like that?' Serres replied, 'He would have noticed that there wasn't an Egyptologist.'

And, indeed, what is the point of a philosopher?

Doesn't Serres' reply link beautifully to our current subject, stupidity? At what stage of life, and in what way, should we come into contact with the idiocy, vulgarity and cruel, pathetic stubbornness that are our daily bread and with which we must live? In France there's a kind of debate – we debate everything, here – about the appropriate age to start studying philosophy. At the moment, young people first come across it in the final year of secondary school. But why not earlier? And why not also introduce children to anthropology, and therefore cultural relativism, at the same time?

U. E. | It seems incredible that Germany, the most philosophical country in the world, doesn't teach philosophy at secondary school. In Italy, on the other hand, the influence of idealistic German historicism means that our schools teach a three-year introduction to the history of philosophy, which is very different from what is offered in France, namely an initiation into philosophical thought. I think it's important to have some idea of what philosophers have thought, from the Presocratics to the present day. The only danger is that the unreflecting student might conclude that the latest thinker is correct. But, having no experience of it, I don't know what effect the French method of teaching philosophy has on young people.

J.-C. C. | All I remember from that year was the sense of being completely bewildered. The curriculum was divided into segments: general philosophy, psychology, logic and ethics. But how can there be a philosophy textbook? And anyway, what about the cultures that haven't developed what we call philosophy? That's what I meant just now by saying that anthropology is just as important. The notion of a 'philosophical concept', for instance, is a purely Western one. Try explaining 'concept' to an Indian – even a highly sophisticated one – or 'transcendence' to a Chinese person! But perhaps we should expand the scope of our discussion about education, without of course claiming to resolve it. Since the 'Jules Ferry' reforms in the early 1880s, French schooling has been free of charge, but compulsory for all. This means that the state is forced to teach the same thing to all its citizens without exception, while knowing full well that most of them will drop out partway through, the eventual goal being to select an elite to run the country. And I am the ultimate profiteer of the system: without Jules Ferry, I wouldn't be here talking to you. I would be a penniless old peasant in the South of France. Although, actually, who knows what I would be?

Every education system is by its very nature a reflection of the culture that has given rise to it, developed it and imposed it. And yet France and Italy have changed massively since Jules Ferry's time. During the Third Republic, 75 per cent of French people were still peasants, perhaps another 10–15 per cent were workers, and what we call the elite represented an even smaller percentage. That 75 per cent of peasants has decreased to 3 or 4 per cent, yet our educational principles remain the same. What's more, in Jules Ferry's time, those unable to make the most of their schooling could find work in agriculture, factories, domestic service or as craftspeople. These trades have gradually disappeared, eclipsed by so-called service or management jobs, meaning that those with only a secondary-school education (if that) are left in freefall. There is nothing for them, nothing to cushion that fall. Our society has completely transformed, whereas our education system has remained more or less the same, at least in principle.

Add to this the much greater number of women now entering higher education, and competing with men for the same number of jobs in the traditionally sought-after sectors. Craftsmanship may no longer appeal to the masses, but the occasional person does discover it as a vocation. A few years ago I sat on a committee awarding prizes to the most skilled candidates working in the so-called 'artistic trades' that are the apogee of craftsmanship. The materials and techniques these people used, and the talent with which they mastered them, were quite astonishing. In this field, at least, nothing has been lost.

U.E. | Yes, in our societies everyone has to grapple with the issue of employment, and some young people are rediscovering cottage industries and traditional crafts. This has certainly been the case in Italy, and I'm sure in France and other Western countries as well. When these new craftsmen and women notice the name on my credit card, it is often obvious that they've read my books. Fifty years ago the same craftspeople wouldn't have finished their education and therefore probably wouldn't have read those books. These contemporary craftspeople have therefore completed higher education before pursuing a manual career.

A friend was telling me how he and a philosophical colleague once took a taxi to Princeton University in New York. The driver, whom my friend described as a bear of a fellow with long shaggy hair, started up a conversation. His passengers explained that they taught at Princeton. The driver wanted to know more. The colleague rather irritably replied that he worked on 'phenomenological reduction through epoché' . . . only for the driver to interrupt with, 'You mean Husserl, right?'

He was of course a philosophy student paying for his studies by driving a cab. At the time, a cab driver

224

who'd heard of Husserl was a rare phenomenon, but these days it wouldn't be particularly surreal to get a ride from someone who played classical music and asked you about your latest book on semiotics.

J.-C. C. | But overall this is good news, wouldn't you say? It even seems to me that the far-from-negligible ecological dangers we are up against may sharpen our intelligence and stop us from remaining too long and too deeply asleep.

U.E. | We can emphasise the obvious positive developments in culture, and the way it is reaching previously excluded social groups. But there is also more stupidity now. The fact that in the old days the peasants kept quiet didn't mean that they were stupid. Being cultured doesn't necessarily make you intelligent. No. But these days everyone wants to be heard, and inevitably in some cases all that is heard is their stupidity. Let's just say that the old kind of stupidity didn't flaunt itself, didn't make itself known, whereas today it shouts from the rooftops.

And yet we must be circumspect about this dividing line between intelligence and stupidity. When it comes to changing a light bulb, I'm a total simpleton. Do the French have those jokes about 'How many . . . does it take to change a light bulb'? No? In Italy we have a whole series. The protagonists used to be the good burghers of Cuneo, a town in Piedmont. 'How many people from Cuneo does it take to change a light bulb?' The answer is five: one to hold the light bulb and four to rotate the table. But the Americans have that joke too. 'How many Californians does it take to change a light bulb? Fifteen: one to change the light bulb and fourteen to share the experience.'

J.-C. C. | You mention people from Cuneo. Cuneo is in the north of Italy. It seems to me that every nation thinks the stupidest people live in the north.

U. E. | Of course, because the mountains that symbolise isolation are found in the north, most people suffering from goitres live in the north, and the barbarians that attacked the cities always came from the north. It's the revenge of the southerners, who have less money and are more technically backward. When the head of the racist Northern League, Umberto Bossi, came 'down' to Rome for the first time to make a speech, protestors waved banners proclaiming, 'We were already poofs when you were still living in trees.'

Southerners have always mocked northerners for being uncultured. Culture is sometimes the last resort of the technologically frustrated. Italians have now replaced people from Cuneo with *carabinieri*, but our

226

police have been clever enough to make the most of this typecasting, which is actually proof of their intelligence.

After the police, it was the turn of the footballer Francesco Totti. He reacted superbly, publishing a book of all the stories and jokes that had been told against him and giving the proceeds to charity. The jokes dried up of their own accord and people soon changed their minds about him.

The Internet, or the
impossibility of *damnatio memoriae*

J.-P. DE T. | What did you think of the banning of *The Satanic Verses*? Isn't the fact that a religious authority managed to ban a book published in England rather alarming?

U. E. | On the contrary, I think the Salman Rushdie case was a cause for great optimism. Why? Because in the past, a book condemned by a religious authority would have had no chance of escaping censorship. The author would almost certainly have been burned at the stake, or stabbed to death. In our age of global communications Rushdie survived, protected by Western intellectuals, and his book survived too.

J.-C. C. | And yet the huge turnout for Rushdie has not been repeated for other authors who have been the subject of a fatwa, and they have been killed, especially in the Middle East. All we can say is that writing has always been, and continues to be, a dangerous practice.

U. E. | I am nevertheless convinced that, in this age of globalisation, we are pretty much informed about everything that is happening, and can therefore act accordingly. Could the Holocaust have happened if the Internet had already existed? I'm not sure. The whole world would immediately have known what was going on. It's the same with China. The Chinese leaders do their utmost to control Internet access, but information still flows in both directions. The Chinese can find out what is happening in the rest of the world. And we can find out what's happening in China.

J.-C. C. | To clarify the situation with regard to Internet censorship, the Chinese have created extremely sophisticated procedures, but they are fallible – simply because Net users will always find a way round them eventually. In China, just like everywhere else, people use their mobile phones to film the things they see, and then send these images around the world. It is going to become harder and harder to hide anything. For dictators, the future is bleak. If they are to succeed, they will have to operate in total darkness.

U. E. | I'm thinking, for example, about the fate of Aung San Suu Kyi. It is much harder for the Junta to kill her now that she is the object of almost universal care and concern. The same went for Íngrid Betancourt, when she was kidnapped by the FARC.

J.-C. C. | I would hate, however, to give the impression that the world has done away with censorship and high-handed behaviour. That is far from being the case.

U.E. | And in any case, even if there were no more censorship through subtraction, it is hard to eliminate censorship through addition – which is how the media do it. Let's imagine a politician writing to a newspaper to explain that he is not guilty of the corruption of which he has been accused; the paper publishes the letter, but manages to place it next to a photo of the author stuffing his face with food. Job done: we have in front of us an image of a man devouring public funds. But more is possible. Say I'm a politician who knows that there will be a very embarrassing story about me on the front pages of tomorrow's papers; I can have a bomb left in the main station that night, and the morning's headlines will be different.

I do wonder if that isn't what's going on with some of the bombings. Not that I want to get involved in conspiracy theories about the 9/11 bombings. There are already plenty of people getting very worked up on that score.

J.-C.C. | It is impossible to believe that a government could have accepted the death of 3,000 of its citizens to cover up some sort of intrigue. It's inconceivable. But there's a very famous example of a cover-up in France – the case of Ben Barka. The Moroccan politician Mehdi Ben Barka is kidnapped in front of the Brasserie Lipp in France, and almost certainly assassinated. General de Gaulle calls a press conference at the Elysée. All the journalists are there. Question: 'Sir, how is it that you waited several days after hearing of Mehdi Ben Barka's kidnapping before telling the press?' 'Must be my lack of experience,' replied de Gaulle with a despondent shrug. Everyone laughed, and the issue was settled. In this case, the diversion worked. A joke triumphed over a man's death.

J.-P. DE T. | Are there other forms of censorship made difficult or impossible by the Internet?

U. E. | Think of the Romans' *damnatio memoriae*. This was a posthumous decree, voted on by the Senate, which condemned a person to silence and removal from remembrance. Their name was wiped off the public registers, any statues were destroyed and their date of birth was declared unlucky. The same thing went on under Stalin, when they destroyed photographs of previous leaders who had been exiled or assassinated. That happened to Trotsky. It would be harder, now, to erase someone from a photograph – the original would suddenly pop up on the Internet, and the disappeared person would reappear.

J.-C.C. | But there are cases of 'spontaneous' collective forgetting that, it seems to me, are even more powerful than collective glory. I'm not referring to careful decisions, as in the case of the Roman Senate. There can also be unconscious choices. A kind of indirect revisionism, or velvet expulsion. There is a collective memory, just as there's a collective unconscious and a collective oblivion. A certain person who has 'had his moment of glory' may depart without a murmur, without ostracism or the slightest force. He leaves of his own accord, discreetly, returning to the kingdom of ghosts – like those Italian film directors I was talking about earlier, from the beginning of the twentieth century. And one day it is exactly as if this person – who has departed from our memories, been gently evicted from our history books, our conversations and our commemorations – had never existed.

U. E. | I once knew a famous Italian critic, who people said brought bad luck. He was quite a legend, and in the end probably played off his own reputation. Even today, he is never mentioned in the discussion of certain works on which he definitely had an influence. That's a form of *damnatio memoriae*. Personally, I never avoided mentioning him. Not only am I the world's least superstitious person, I also admired his work too much not to acknowledge it. I even decided

235

to go and visit him once, by plane. When nothing bad happened to me, I was told that I must now be under his protection. Apart from a happy few (including me) who still talk about him, his legacy has indeed been effaced.

J.-C.C. | There are of course several ways to condemn a person, book or culture to silence and oblivion. We've discussed some of them. Systematically destroying a language – as the Spanish did in the Americas – is clearly the most effective way of permanently making the culture it expresses inaccessible, and thus being able to make it say whatever you like. But as we have seen, these cultures and languages resist. It isn't easy to silence a voice definitively, to wipe out a language once and for all; the centuries speak in murmurs. You're right that the Rushdie case gives cause for hope; it is definitely one of the most important achievements of our globalised world. Total, permanent censorship is now almost inconceivable. The only problem is that the news doing the rounds will become impossible to verify. As discussed, one day soon we will all be informants. Willing informants of a more or less qualified, more or less biased nature, who will also, by the same process, have become inventors, creators of news, every day imagining the world anew. It may come to that: describing the world according to our desires, which we will by then take for reality.

236

The only way around this – if we think it necessary, because imagined news would probably have its own charm – would be continual, never-ending cross-checking. What a drag! A single witness isn't enough to establish a fact. The same goes for a crime. There has to be a convergence of perspectives and witness statements. But for the most part, it isn't worth this massive undertaking. So we let it go.

U. E. | But an abundance of witnesses isn't necessarily enough. We witnessed the violence inflicted on Tibetan monks by the Chinese police. It provoked international outrage. But if our screens kept showing monks being beaten by police for months on end, even the most concerned and active audience would lose interest. There is therefore a level below which news pieces do not penetrate and above which they become nothing but background noise.

J.-C. C. | They are like bubbles that inflate and then pop. One year we are in the 'persecuted Tibetan monks' bubble. The next we are moved into the 'Íngrid Betancourt' bubble. Then it becomes the 'subprime crash' bubble, then the banking crisis, or the Stock Market showdown, or both at once. What will the next bubble be? When a predicted mammoth hurricane fails to hit the coast of Florida, journalists seem almost disappointed, but for the inhabitants it's wonderful news.

How is real news constructed from this huge pool of information? How is it that a piece of news can rip around the planet, commanding everyone's attention for a fixed length of time, only to interest no one at all a few days later? For example, when Buñuel and I were in Spain in 1976, working on *That Obscure Object of Desire*, we used to get the papers delivered every day. One day we read that a bomb had exploded in Montmartre's Sacré-Coeur. Nobody had claimed responsibility for the attack, and the police were carrying out an investigation. Astonishment and delight. For Buñuel, this was great news; that someone had planted a bomb in the church of shame, the church actually built to 'expiate the crimes of the communards', was an unhoped-for joy, a godsend. There have, in fact, been many attempts to destroy this dishonouring monument, or else – as the anarchists desired at a certain point – to paint it red.

So the next morning we all grabbed the papers to find out what had happened. Nothing, not even a word. And there never was again. Disappointment and frustration. The only thing to do was incorporate a direct-action group called the 'Revolutionary Army of the Infant Jesus' into our screenplay.

U.E. | Returning to censorship through subtraction, a dictatorship determined to wipe out any hope of accessing sources of information or knowledge online could easily spread a virus that would destroy all the personal data in every computer, and thus create a massive information blackout. Although perhaps the possibility of destroying everything doesn't really exist, as we all keep some of our data on USB sticks. But still. Might this cyber-dictatorship be able to wipe out as much as 80 per cent of our personal data?

J.-C.C. | But perhaps there's no need to destroy everything. Just as I can use the 'Find' function to search a document for every occurrence of a certain word and then wipe them all out with a single click, why couldn't there be a form of IT censorship designed to destroy only a single word or group of words, but on every computer worldwide? But then which words would our dictators choose? And there is bound to be a counterattack by Net users: that always happens. It's the old story of attack and defence, but on new terrain. One can also imagine a new Babel – a sudden disappearance of languages, codes, keys of any kind. What chaos!

J.-P. DET. | The paradox, as you have suggested, is that the work of art or person condemned to silence can make of this silence a kind of echo chamber, thus eventually finding their way back into our memories. Could you give us some examples of these kinds of reversals of fate?

U. E. | It's a different take on *damnatio memoriae*. Let's say that for many and complex reasons – filtering out, accidents, fire – a work of art does not reach us. No one person can truly be blamed for its disappearance. But it is still missing. And because the work has been critiqued and praised by a great many witnesses, its very absence draws attention to it. That's exactly what happened with the work of the ancient Greek painter Zeuxis. No one apart from the artist's contemporaries has ever seen the paintings, and yet we still talk about him today.

J.-C. C. | When Tutankhamun succeeded Akhenaten, they used a chisel to efface from the temples the name of the dead pharaoh, now denounced as a dissenter. And Akhenaten wasn't the only one to be wiped out like that. Inscriptions crumble, statues collapse. Which reminds me of Josef Koudelka's wonderful photograph of a statue of Lenin laid out on a barge like a massive corpse, floating down the Danube towards the Black Sea, where it would disappear.

I should perhaps clarify something about the statues of the Buddha destroyed in Afghanistan. For the first few centuries after his sermons, the Buddha was not depicted. He was portrayed by his absence. Footprints. An empty chair. A tree in the shade of which he used to meditate. A horse with a saddle, but no rider.

It was only after the invasion of Alexander the Great that the people of central Asia, influenced by Greek art, began to give the Buddha a physical form. Therefore the Taliban unwittingly helped return Buddhism to its roots. For true Buddhists, the now-empty alcoves in the Bamiyan Valley are perhaps more eloquent and evocative than they ever were before.

The acts of terrorism to which Arab-Muslim culture can now sometimes seem to be reduced almost manage to obscure its former grandeur, just as for centuries the bloody sacrifices of the Aztecs obscured all the wonders of their civilisation. The Spanish emphasised those sacrifices to such an extent that by the time they wanted to wipe out the remaining traces of the defeated civilisation, the bloody sacrifices were almost the only thing the collective memory had retained. Islam is currently risking this same fate of being reduced, in our short-term memories, to nothing but the terrorist violence. Because our memories, like our minds, are reductive. We are constantly selecting and reducing.

Fire as censor

J. P. DE T. | It must be said that fire has a special place amongst the worst censors in book history.

U. E. | Absolutely – and the first thing to mention are the Nazi bonfires intended to destroy 'degenerate' books.

J.-C. C. | In *Fahrenheit 451* Ray Bradbury describes a society that wants to free itself from the burdensome legacy of books, and decides to burn them all. Paper burns at exactly 451 degrees Fahrenheit, as the firefighters find out because the job of burning the books is given to them.

U. E. | There's also an Italian radio programme called *Fahrenheit 451*. But it's exactly the opposite: listeners phone in to say that they haven't been able to find, or have lost, such and such a book, and then other listeners phone in to say they have a copy they're willing to lend. It's like leaving a book you've read in a cinema or on the Underground, so that someone else will have the pleasure of finding it. But, to return to the point, accidental and intentional fires have been part of book history since the very beginning. It would be impossible to list all the libraries that have burned down.

J.-C. C. | I'm reminded of an event I was invited to one night at the Louvre. Each of us had to pick one of the paintings and talk about it to a small group of people. I chose a painting called *Saint Paul preaching at Ephesus* by the early seventeenth-century French artist Eustache Le Sueur. It shows a bearded St Paul wearing a robe: the spitting image of one of today's ayatollahs, but without the turban. His eyes are blazing. A few believers are listening. In the fore-ground of the painting a black servant is on his knees burning books. I went right up close to see what books were being burned. I could just make out numbers and mathematical formulae on the pages. So the probably just-converted slave was burning books on Greek science. What was the overt or covert message that the painter was trying to convey? I can't say. But it's still a very striking image. With the arrival of faith, science is destroyed. That is more than filtering out, it's erasure by way of fire. The square of the hypotenuse must disappear for ever.

U. E. | There's even a racist aspect, because the task of burning the books is given to a black man. We are pretty sure that the Nazis burned more books than anyone else. But how much do we really know about what happened during the Crusades?

J.-C. C. | I think that the Spanish in the New World were actually worse book-destroyers than the Nazis. The Mongols didn't pull their punches, either.

U. E. | At the dawn of modernity, the Western world came into contact with two as-yet-unknown cultures, the Chinese and the Amerindian. China was a great empire that could neither be conquered nor colonised, but with which one could trade. The Jesuits went there on a mission not to convert, but rather to encourage a dialogue between the cultures and religions. The Amerindian world seemed, on the other hand, to be populated by bloodthirsty savages, and therefore fell victim to both wholesale looting and a horrific genocide. The ideological justification for this contrasting behaviour was based on the nature of the languages used in each place. The Amerindian pictographs were defined as simple copies of things arising in the environment and thus lacking any conceptual status, whereas the Chinese ideograms represented ideas and were thus more 'philosophical'. We now know that the pictographic writing was much more sophisticated than they thought. How many pictographic texts have been lost in this way?

J.-C. C. | As they destroyed the remains of those remarkable civilisations, the Spanish had no idea of the treasures

247

that they were burning. Having said that, some of them – in particular the remarkable monk Bernardino de Sahagún – did sense that there was something there that must not be destroyed, something that made up an essential part of what we think of today as our cultural heritage.

U. E. | The Jesuits who went to China were well-educated men, whereas Cortés and especially Pizarro were butchers driven by a mission to destroy a culture. And the Franciscans who went with them thought of the natives as wild animals.

J.-C. C. | Not all of them, thank God. Sahagún, Las Casas and Durán were all exceptions, often at serious risk to their own lives. We owe to them everything we know about the lives of the Indians before the conquest.

U. E. | Sahagún was a Franciscan, but Las Casas and Durán were Dominicans. It's interesting how wrong clichés can be. Supposedly the Dominicans were the inquisitors, whereas the Franciscans were the epitome of gentleness. And yet what happened in Latin America was almost like a Western movie – the Franciscans played the bad guys and, sometimes, the Dominicans would play the good guys.

J.-P. DET. | Why did the Spanish destroy some pre-Columbian buildings and spare others?

J.-C. C. | Some they simply didn't see. That was the case with the great Mayan cities, which had been abandoned several centuries earlier and were already reclaimed by the jungle. The same goes for Teotihuacán, further north. The city had already been deserted by the time the Aztecs arrived in the area around the thirteenth century.

The mania for wiping out every written trace shows how the invaders considered a people without writing a people forever cursed. In Bulgaria, they've recently discovered silverwork in graves known to be from the second or third millennium BC. And yet the Thracians, like the Gauls, didn't leave any written traces, and peoples without writing – who did not name themselves and did not tell their stories (even inaccurately) – those peoples did not exist, even if their silver-smithing was superb and very refined. If you want someone to remember you, you had better write. Write and make sure that your writings aren't destroyed in someone's fire. I sometimes wonder what the Nazis were thinking when they burned Jewish books. Were they hoping to destroy them all, right down to the last one? Wouldn't that be more criminal than utopian?

So it seems to me their mission was more symbolic in nature.

I am also surprised and appalled by some of the other kinds of manipulation that take place today, under our very eyes. Given that I visit Iran on a fairly regular basis, I once suggested to a well-known film company that I take a small crew with me to film my impressions of the country. The director of the company called me to a meeting and started by telling me how he perceived the country, despite the fact that he didn't know it. He told me precisely what I should film. It would be he who would decide what images I brought back from a country he had never visited: chest-beating fundamentalists, drug addicts, prostitutes, and so on. Needless to say, the film was never made.

We see every day how misleading images can be. These subtle falsifications are all the more difficult to spot because they are presented as 'images', or in other words documentary data. But in the end, whether we believe it or not, nothing is easier to misrepresent than the truth.

I remember watching a TV documentary about Kabul. I know Kabul. Every shot was filmed from below, so that you saw only the war-mangled tops of the houses, and nothing of the streets, the shops or the passers-by. And all the interviews were with people who talked about the dreadful state of the country. Every one of them. The only soundtrack to the entire programme was a creepy wind noise, the kind of thing you might hear in desert films, but on a loop. It had obviously been found in a sound-effects library and popped in here and there – regardless of the fact that the very light clothes people were wearing weren't even fluttering. That film was a complete lie. Yet again.

U. E. | The Russian film-maker Lev Kuleshov was one of the first to show how images infect each other and how one can make them say very different things. The viewer will go away with one impression if you show a man's face just after an image of a lovely plate of food, and a completely different impression if you show it straight after something revolting. In the first case, the man's face expresses appetite, in the second disgust.

J.-C. C. | Our eyes end up seeing what the images want us to see. At the end of Polanski's *Rosemary's Baby*, lots of people saw the monstrous baby, because he was described by the characters leaning over his crib. But in fact Polanski never filmed the baby.

U. E. | Lots of people probably also saw the contents of the notorious oriental box in *Belle de Jour*.

J.-C.C. | Of course. When Buñuel was asked what was inside, he would always say: 'A photo of Mr Carrière. That's why the girls are so horrified.' One day a stranger phoned me at home. He was calling about that film, and wanted to know if I had ever lived in Laos. I told him I'd never set foot in the country. He asked the same question about Buñuel and I gave the same answer. The man on the phone seemed astonished. The notorious box had reminded him of an ancient Laotian custom. So I asked him if he knew what was inside the box. 'Of course!' he said, and I replied, 'Well then, would you be so kind as to tell me?' He explained that in this custom the women use silver chains to position large scarab beetles over their clitorises during lovemaking, to make their orgasms slower and more delicate. I was completely taken aback, and told him that we'd never thought of shutting a scarab beetle inside the *Belle de Jour* box. The man hung up. And I was suddenly terribly disappointed by the idea of knowing. The bittersweet delight of the mystery was gone.

All this is to say that the image – in which we often see something other than what is actually shown – can lie in a much more subtle way than written or spoken language. If we want to keep our visual memory in any way intact, we must teach the coming generations how to look at images. That's a real priority.

U. E. | And now we're prey to another form of censorship. We can preserve every book in the world, maintain every digital format and every archive, but if some kind of mass crisis suddenly renders untranslatable all the languages we have chosen for the conservation of this massive cultural legacy, then that legacy will be irrevocably lost.

J.-C. C. | That's what happened with hieroglyphic writing. Theodosius I decreed in 380 that the Christian religion was the single official state religion, and compulsory throughout the Empire. The Egyptian temples were closed, among others. The priests, who were the experts on and depositaries of that writing, found themselves unable to transmit their knowledge. They were forced to bury the gods with whom they had been living for millennia. And along with the gods, their liturgical objects and the language itself. It took only a single generation for all of that to be destroyed. Seemingly for ever.

U. E. | It took fourteen centuries for us to rediscover the key to that language.

J.-P. DE T. | Let's go back to censorship by fire for a moment. Those who burned down ancient libraries may have thought they had destroyed every trace of the manuscripts in those libraries. But since the invention of printing, that is no longer possible. You can burn one, two or even a hundred copies of a printed book without in any way removing the book from existence. Other copies can probably still be found in many, many other public and private libraries. So what is the point of modern book-burning, as practised for example by the Nazis?

U. E. | The censor knows full well that he is not destroying every copy of the banned book. But it's a way of setting himself up as a demiurge capable of consuming the world – a whole conception of the world – by fire. The alibi, of course, is regeneration; the purification of a culture poisoned by certain books. It's no accident that the Nazis spoke of 'degenerate art'. The auto-da-fé is a kind of curative treatment.

J.-C. C. | This image of publication, dissemination, conservation and destruction is well illustrated by the Hindu god Shiva. Shiva dances within a ring of fire. To the beat of the drum in his right hand, the universe is created, while the flame in his left sparks the destruction of all that surrounds him. Each hand is of equal value.

254

U. E. | That isn't too far from the ideas of Heraclitus, and the Stoics. Everything is born from fire, and fire destroys everything so that everything may become one again. People have always preferred to burn heretics than cut off their heads, which would be a much easier and quicker solution. The burning sends out a message to those with the same ideas or who own the same books.

J.-C. C. | Let's take Goebbels, probably the only Nazi intellectual who also loved collecting books. You're right to say that those who burn books know exactly what they're doing. You have to respect a book's power to want to destroy it. At the same time, the censor is not insane. He knows that he is not going to destroy a blacklisted book by burning a few copies. But the act is still highly symbolic. Most importantly, it says to others: you too may burn this book. Don't hesitate. It's a good thing to do.

J.-P. DE T. | Rather like burning the American flag in Tehran, or somewhere like that . . .

J.-C. C. | Quite. A single burnt flag can represent the determination of a movement, or even a whole people. And yet, as we have seen so many times, fire can never

255

reduce everything to silence. Even amongst the Spanish, who were determined to eradicate every trace of several cultures, there were certain monks who tried to save a few specimens. Bernardino de Sahagún – whom we have already mentioned, but who can never be mentioned too many times – asked the Aztecs to copy out (often in secret) books that were being thrown on the fire in other places. He asked indigenous painters to illustrate them. But the poor man never saw his work published, because the authorities seized it. Sahagún was so naïve that he even offered to hand over his drafts as well. Luckily, that didn't happen. And those drafts were the main source for the publication of almost everything we know about the Aztecs, two centuries later.

U. E. | It took the Spanish quite a long time to destroy the remains of a civilisation. But Nazism only lasted twelve years.

J.-C. C. | And Napoleon eleven. And Bush eight. Not that they are comparable, of course. As I've said, I once focused, 'for fun', on twenty years of twentieth-century history, from Hitler's ascent to power in 1933 to Stalin's death in 1953. Just think of everything that happened during those twenty years. The Second World War, and as if that weren't enough, huge numbers of lesser wars before, during and after: the Spanish Civil War, the war in Ethiopia, the Korean War . . . I'll miss some out, I'm sure. It's the return of Shiva. I mentioned two of his four hands. Everything that is born shall be destroyed. But the third hand is in the position of *abaya*, meaning 'fear not', because of his fourth hand signifying 'with the force of my mind I've already lifted one of my feet from the ground'. It's one of the most complex images that humanity has ever produced. Compared with it, Christ on his cross – the image of a dying man to which our culture has bowed down – seems rather simple. Although, paradoxically, that may be what has made it so powerful.

U. E. | Allow me to return to the Nazis. There's something strange about their crusade against books. The designer of the Nazis' cultural policies was Goebbels, who understood the new methods of information-dissemination very well, and realised that radio would soon become the primary medium of communication. Using the power of the media to destroy the power of books – now that was prophetic.

J.-C. C. | How did we humans go from Nazi book-burning to Mao's Little Red Book, and the fervour that gripped a nation of one billion human beings for several years?

U. E. | Mao's genius was first to make the Little Red Book a kind of flag to brandish. There was no need to actually read it. Secondly, he realised that sacred texts are never read from beginning to end, so made it a collection of little stand-alone extracts, aphorisms that could be learned by heart and recited like mantras or litanies.

J.-C. C. | But how did they get to this seemingly idiotic nationwide obsession with brandishing a red book? Why did this collectivist Marxist regime make a book its primary symbol?

U. E. | While it was going on, we knew hardly anything about the Cultural Revolution and the ways in which the masses were being manipulated. In 1971 I contributed to a book about Chinese comics. A journalist based in China had collected together all kinds of material: comic books in the English style, but also photo stories. The comics had been created during the Cultural Revolution, but they gave no indication whatsoever of what was happening in China at the time. On the contrary, they were pacifist – against violence of any sort, and encouraging tolerance and mutual understanding. It was the same with the Little Red Book, which appeared as a symbol of non-violence. Nothing, of course, was said about the fact that the glorification of *that* little book implied the destruction of all others.

J.-C. C. | I was in China when Bertolucci was filming *The Last Emperor*. I was writing three different articles – one on the film itself, another on the renaissance of Chinese film for *Cahiers du Cinéma*, and a third on the relearning of traditional Chinese musical instruments for a French music magazine. The most memorable interview was the one with the director of the Institute of Traditional Musical Instruments. I wanted to find out how it was that people had stopped playing these instruments during the Cultural Revolution. He was only just becoming able to speak a little more freely. He told me that first of all they closed the Institute and destroyed the library. At some risk to his life, he managed to save a few works by sending them to relatives in the countryside. Then he was transferred to a village to work in the fields. Everyone with a specialism or particular knowledge had to be neutralised. That was the basic principle of the Revolution: all knowledge has inherent power, so knowledge must be destroyed.

The man turned up in a peasant community, where they could immediately see he had no idea how to use a spade or a pickaxe. So they told him to stay at home. And this man, the world expert on Chinese

259

traditional music, told me: 'For nine years, I played dominos.'

We don't need to go back to the Spanish in the Americas four or five centuries ago, or to the massacres that the Christians committed during the Crusades. No. We can talk about what has happened during our own lifetimes. And we can never be sure that the worst is behind us. In his *A Universal History of the Destruction of Books*, Fernando Báez draws our attention to the destruction of the Baghdad Library as recently as 2003. That wasn't of course the first attempt to destroy a Baghdad library. The Mongols had already tried. That land has been invaded and looted so many times, but little green shoots always reappear. In the tenth, eleventh and twelfth centuries, Muslim civilisation was undoubtedly the most impressive in the world. But then it was suddenly attacked, from both sides. By the Christian Crusades and also by the Mongols, who took Baghdad in the thirteenth century and razed it to the ground. As we've said, the Mongols destroyed things blindly, but the Christians weren't much better. Báez writes that they destroyed about three million books during their stay in the Holy Land.

U.E. | That's right – the arrival of the Crusaders pretty much destroyed Jerusalem.

J.-C. C. | The same thing happened during the Spanish Reconquista at the end of the fifteenth century. Queen Isabella of Castile's advisor Cardinal Jiménez de Cisneros ordered the burning of all books found in Granada, with the exception of a few works of medicine. Báez says that half the Sufi poems of the era were burned at that time. We shouldn't always claim that it's others who burn our books. We have certainly done our fair share of destroying knowledge and beauty.

Having said that, let's lighten up this catalogue of woe by remembering that some of the worst enemies of books have – surprisingly – been authors themselves. And not so far from our shores. Philippe Sollers tells us of a Student-Writer Action Committee in the French upheavals of 1968, which I hadn't heard of before and which sounds rather farcical. It protested energetically against traditional education (quite normal for the time) and asked, not without pretension, for a 'new knowledge'. Maurice Blanchot was a vociferous part of this committee. Its main demand was for the overthrow of the book, which according to them held knowledge prisoner. Words had to liberate themselves from the book, from the book as object, and escape. Where to? Nobody said. But still they wrote: 'No more books, no more books ever!' Slogans that were written and put forward by writers!

U.E. | To conclude this business of book-burners, we should mention the authors who have tried, and sometimes managed, to set fire to their own work . . .

J.-C.C. | This obsession with destroying that which has been created must come from deep within us. Think of Kafka's crazy deathbed compulsion to burn his work. Rimbaud wanted to destroy *A Season in Hell*. And Borges actually did destroy his early books.

U.E. | On his deathbed, Virgil asked for *The Aeneid* to be burned. Who knows whether these dreams of destruction aren't partly the archetypal notion of a death through fire that would bring forth the birth of a new world? Or, on the other hand, the notion that I die and the world dies with me . . . as with Hitler committing suicide after having sent the world up in flames.

J.-C.C. | When Shakespeare's Timon of Athens dies, he cries: 'Sun, hide thy beams. Timon hath done his reign.' Reminiscent of a kamikaze dragging a part of the rejected world down with him when he dies. But actually both suicide bombers and Japanese kamikazes flying into American flotillas are dying for a cause. I said somewhere that Samson was the first kamikaze. He caused the collapse of the temple in which he was imprisoned, killing a great many Philistines along with himself. Suicide bombs are both crime and punishment. I once worked with the Japanese film-maker Nagisa Oshima. He told me that, at some point in his life, every Japanese comes very close to both the thought and the act of suicide.

U. E. | Like the suicide of Jim Jones and almost a thousand of his disciples in Guyana. And the collective death of the Davidians in Waco in 1993.

J.-C. C. | It's worth rereading Corneille's *Polyeuctus* from time to time. It describes the life of a Christian convert under the Roman Empire, who wants to martyr himself, and his wife Pauline, too. For him there is no greater destiny. How's that for a wedding present?

J.-P. DE T. | We're starting to see that writing a book, having it published and selling lots of copies isn't necessarily the surest way to go down in history . . .

U. E. | Quite. One way for a person to make their name is through creativity (in the realms of art, politics or thought). But if they are unable to create, there's always destruction – of a work of art or sometimes themselves. Erostratus, for example, made his name by destroying

the Artemis temple at Ephesus. The Athenian government knew that he had set fire to it with the sole aim
of going down in history, so they forbade his name
to be spoken. Which obviously didn't work – the proof
being that we still know Erostratus' name, whereas
we've forgotten who built that temple at Ephesus. And
Erostratus has many heirs, of course. Including all the
people who go on TV to tell us their partners are
cheating on them. A modern form of self-destruction.
They'll do anything to get on TV. Like the serial killer
who actually wants to be caught, so that people will
be talking about him.

J.-C. C. | Andy Warhol encapsulated this desire in his well-
known statement 'In the future, everyone will be world-
famous for fifteen minutes.'

U. E. | It's the same instinct that makes some guy, who
happens to be standing behind someone being filmed
for TV, wave his arms around so as to be seen. It might
seem idiotic to us, but it's his moment of glory.

J.-C. C. | People approach TV programme makers with all
kinds of wild offers. Some even say they want to kill
themselves live on TV. Or be shown in pain, being
whipped or tortured. Or screen their wife making love

with another man. The varieties of contemporary exhibitionism seem to be endless.

U. E. | There's a programme on Italian TV called *La Corrida*, in which amateurs perform to the boos of the crowd. They all know they're going to be torn to pieces and yet the programme is inundated with candidates. Very few of them are under the illusion that they have any talent; they're just willing to do anything for this unique chance to be seen by millions of people.

All the books we haven't read

J.-P. DE T. | You've mentioned a great many diverse and strange-sounding books during these interviews, but allow me to ask you one question: have you read them? Must an educated man necessarily have read the books he is supposed to know? Or is it enough for him to form an opinion that, once firmly established, excuses him from ever having to read the actual books? I'm sure you've heard of Pierre Bayard's book *How to Talk about Books You Haven't Read*. So, please tell me about the books that you haven't read . . .

U. E. | I'll start, if you like. Pierre Bayard and I once did a public debate in New York, and I think he has some interesting things to say on the matter. There are more books in the world than hours in which to read them. And that doesn't just apply to all the books ever published, but even to only the most important books of a particular culture. We are thus deeply influenced by books that we haven't read, that we haven't had the time to read. Who has actually read *Finnegans Wake* – I mean from beginning to end? Who has read the Bible properly, from Genesis to the Apocalypse? If I were to combine all the sections I've read, I could boast of about one-third. But no more.

And yet I've a fairly accurate notion of what I haven't read.

I have to admit that I only read *War and Peace* when I was forty. But I knew the basics before then. You've mentioned the Mahabharata – I've never read that, despite owning three editions in three different languages. Who's read *The Thousand and One Nights* from beginning to end? Who has actually read the *Kama Sutra*? And yet everyone talks about it, and some practise it too. So we can see that the world is full of books that we haven't read, but that we know pretty well. The question therefore is how we have come to know these books. Bayard says he has never read Joyce's *Ulysses*, but knows it well enough to teach to his students. He can tell them that the book tells the story of a single day, is set in Dublin, has a Jewish protagonist, makes use of the interior monologue, etc. And all these elements are absolutely true, despite him not having read it.

There are several ways of responding to the person who comes to your house, notices your impressive library and can only think to ask, 'Have you read them all?' One of my friends used to say, 'And more, my dear sir, and more.'

Personally, I've two replies. The first: 'No. These are just the books I'm planning to read next week. The ones I've already read are at the university.' The second:

'I haven't read any of these books. Why would I keep them, otherwise?' There are of course more contentious responses, if you're willing to further antagonise and even anger your guest. The truth is that we all own dozens, or hundreds, or even thousands (in the case of an extensive library) of books that we haven't read. And yet when we eventually pick them up, we find that they are already familiar. How is that? How do we already know the books that we haven't read? Firstly, there's the esoteric explanation – there are these waves that somehow travel from the book to you – to which I don't subscribe. Secondly, perhaps it's not true that you've never opened the book; over the years you're bound to have moved it from place to place, and may in the process have flicked through it and forgotten that you've done so. Thirdly, over the years you've read lots of books that have mentioned this one and so made it seem familiar. There are thus several ways to know something of books that we haven't read. Which is a good thing – otherwise how would one ever find time to read the same book four times?

J.-C. C. | There are books on our shelves that we haven't read and doubtless never will, that each of us has probably put to one side in the belief that we will read them later on, much later, perhaps even in another life. The terrible grief of the dying as they realise their

271

last hour is upon them and they still haven't read Proust.

U. E. | When people ask me whether I've read this or that book, I've found that a safe answer is, 'You know, I don't read, I write.' That shuts them up. Although some of the questions come up time and time again: 'Have you read Thackeray's novel *Vanity Fair*?' I ended up giving in and trying to read it, on three different occasions. But I found it terribly dull.

J.-C. C. | I'd promised myself I would read it, so you've just done me a great service. Thank you.

U. E. | When I was at the University of Turin, I lived in the halls of residence. We used to slip a coin to the leader of the applause at the local theatre, and he would let us watch the plays. In those four years of university I saw every masterpiece of ancient and contemporary theatre. However, the play rarely finished in time for us to get back to our rooms before the doors closed at half-past midnight, so I saw them all minus the final five or ten minutes. Later on I met my friend Paolo Fabbri, and he told me that as a student he used to make a bit of cash selling tickets at the Urbino university theatre. So he didn't get in to the show until the audience were all in, quarter of an hour after the curtain went up. He used to miss the beginning, and I the end. We needed to help each other out – something we've always dreamed of doing.

J.-C. C. | In a similar way, I sometimes wonder if I've actually seen all the films I think I've seen. Perhaps I've just seen extracts on TV, or read books that mention them. I know the plot, friends have talked about them. There's a confusion in my mind between the films I'm sure I've seen, the films I know I haven't seen and all the others. For instance Fritz Lang's silent film *Die Nibelungen*: I can see images of Siegfried killing the dragon in a magnificent studio forest. The trees look as if they're made of cement. But have I seen the whole film? Or only that scene? Then there are the films I'm sure I haven't seen, but talk about as if I have. Sometimes with rather too much authority. I remember being in Rome once with Louis Malle and some French and Italian friends. We started talking about Luchino Visconti's film *The Leopard*. Louis and I disagreed and, both being professionals in the field, did our best to win the argument. One of us loved the film and the other loathed it – I can't remember which was which, and it doesn't matter. The whole table was listening. I was suddenly paralysed by doubt, and asked Louis, 'But have you seen it?' He replied, 'No, have you?' – 'Me neither'. The people listening were quite upset, they thought we'd been wasting their time.

U. E. | When a chair falls vacant at one of the Italian universities, a national commission meets to appoint the best person to the job. Each commissioner receives great piles of publications by each of the candidates. There's a story about one of the commissioners sitting in his office surrounded by all these documents. He is asked when he will find time to read them, and he replies, 'I won't ever read them. I can't let myself be influenced by the people I'm supposed to be assessing.'

J.-C. C. | He was quite right. Once you've read a book, or seen a film, you find yourself having to defend your personal opinion, whereas if you know nothing about the work, then you select the very best of everyone else's diverse opinions, cherry-picking the most convincing arguments, combating your natural laziness and even your own taste, which may not necessarily be right . . .

There's another problem. Let's take the example of Kafka's *The Castle*, which I read a long time ago. Since then, I've seen two very loose film adaptations including Michael Haneke's, and they have seriously altered my first impression, and inevitably blurred my memory of the book. When I think of *The Castle*, won't it now always be through those film-makers' eyes? You say that the Shakespeare plays we read today are necessarily richer than the plays he actually wrote, because of all the great readings and interpretations they have absorbed since Shakespeare's quill scratched rapidly across the paper. And I think you're right. Shakespeare is growing richer and more substantial all the time.

U. E. | I've explained how in Italy young people discover philosophy through its history, rather than through philosophical reflection as in France. My philosophy teacher was a remarkable man, and it was because of him that I studied philosophy at university. His efforts actually enabled me to understand some aspects of philosophy. It seems likely that this superb teacher hadn't been able to read all the books he mentioned in his classes. Which means that he probably didn't know a lot of the books he talked about so knowledgeably and enthusiastically. He knew them only through the history of philosophy.

J.-C. C. | When Emmanuel Le Roy Ladurie was running the Bibliothèque nationale, he commissioned a remarkable study, which found that more than two million of the library's books hadn't been requested since it was first conceived of during the Revolution, or let's say from the 1820s. Not even once. Perhaps they are all quite devoid of interest – devotional books, prayer anthologies, the kind of bad science you're so keen on, thinkers that have rightly been forgotten. When

275

they were first creating the library's collection, cart-loads of jumbled-up books were deposited in the court-yard of the rue de Richelieu. They all had to be received and categorised, probably in a great rush. Then most of them fell into a deep sleep from which they have not yet awoken.

It is hardly comforting for the author or writer – so for the three of us – to think of our books gathering dust on a shelf without anyone ever taking them down. Although I can't imagine that's the case with your books, Umberto. Which country likes them the best?

U. E. | Probably Germany, in terms of sales. In France, selling 200,000 or 300,000 copies is a big deal. In Germany you have to sell more than one million to make a splash. The lowest sales are in England. The English mostly prefer to borrow their books from libraries. As for Italy, sales are probably slightly higher than in Ghana. Instead of books, Italians read a lot of magazines – many more than the French. But the newspapers have discovered a great way to encourage non-readers to read. It's been done in Spain and Italy, but not in France. The newspaper offers its readers a free book or DVD with the very modest price of the paper. The bookshops fought this practice, but it now happens all the time. On the day *The Name of the Rose* was offered free with *La*

Repubblica, the paper sold two million copies instead of the usual 650,000: my book therefore reached two million readers (and if you think that the book might be read by the whole family, that figure could easily reach four million).

It's easy to understand how that could upset booksellers. And yet, when they came to check the next biannual sales figures, they found that sales of the paperback had only decreased very slightly. Those two million must therefore not have been people who regularly visit bookshops. We had acquired a new readership.

J. P. DE T. | Both of you seem very enthusiastic about the practice of reading in our societies. Reading is no longer merely the province of the elite. Despite competition from various increasingly appealing and impressive media, books emerge unscathed, proving that they cannot be replaced. The wheel is, once again, unsurpassable.

J.-C. C. | One day, about twenty years ago, I was taking the metro from Hôtel-de-Ville. There was a bench on the platform, and on the bench was a man with four or five books piled up next to him. The man was reading. The trains were coming and going. I watched this man, who was taking no notice of anything but his books, and decided to wait for a while. I was fascinated. In the end I walked up to him and we had a brief conversation. I asked him in a friendly way what he was doing there. He told me that he arrived at eight o'clock every morning, and stayed there till noon. He went out for an hour to have lunch. Then he returned to his bench and stayed there till 6 p.m. He finished with these unforgettable words: 'I read, I've never done anything else.' I left, feeling that I was wasting his time.

Why in the metro? Because he wouldn't have been able to sit in a café all day without eating or drinking, and he obviously couldn't afford to do that. The metro was free, warm and he wasn't in the least bothered by all the comings and goings. I wondered then, and I still wonder now, whether he was the perfect reader, or utterly perverse.

U. E. | And what was he reading?

J.-C. C. | It was very eclectic. Novels, history books, essays. It seems to me that he was more dependent on the fact of reading than actually interested in the material. It has been said that reading is an unpunished vice. This example shows that it can become a perversion. A fetish, even.

U. E. | When I was a child, one of our neighbours used to give me a book every Christmas. One day she asked, 'Umbertino, do you read to find out what happens in the book, or for the love of reading?' And I had to admit that I wasn't always particularly fascinated by what I was reading. I was reading for the love of it; anything would do. That was a big childhood revelation.

J.-C. C. | Reading for the sake of reading, like living for the sake of living. There are also people who go to the cinema for the sake of seeing films, in the sense of moving images. Sometimes it doesn't much matter what the film shows or portrays.

J.-P. DE T. | Has anyone managed to diagnose an addiction to reading?

J.-C. C. | Of course. That man in the metro was addicted. Imagine someone who spent several hours a day walking, without paying any attention to the landscape, the people he met or the air he breathed. There is the pure activity of reading, just as there is of walking and running. What can you retain of books you've read in that way? How can you remember what you've read when you've read two or three books that day? Some people shut themselves up in the cinema and watch four or five films in succession. Journalists and juries have to do it during film festivals, and it's hard to keep your bearings.

U. E. | I did that once, when I was on the Venice Film Festival jury. I thought I was going mad.

J.-C. C. | You stagger out of the projection room at Cannes having seen your daily ration, and even the palm trees on La Croisette look fake. The aim isn't to read at any cost, or watch at any cost, but to know how to turn the activity into something nourishing and sustainable. Do those who read very fast actually taste what they are reading? If you skip over the long descriptions in Balzac, aren't you missing precisely what makes his work so deeply resonant? And so unique?

U. E. | Like people who look for the speech marks when they're reading, so they can skip to the dialogue. As a child, I sometimes skipped certain passages to get to the next bit of dialogue in my adventure stories.

But let's keep on exploring this theme of the books we haven't read. There is another way of encouraging people to read, as imagined by the author Achille Campanile when he tells the story of how the Marquis Fuscaldo became the most educated man of his time. The marquis inherited a massive library from his father, but had no interest in it whatsoever. One day he happened to flick through one of the books and found a 1,000-lire note between two pages. Hoping to repeat the experience, he spent the rest of his life paging through every one of the books he had inherited. And thus became a fount of knowledge.

J.-P. DE T. | 'Do not read Anatole France!' Surely advising or 'dis-advising' us to read something, as the Surrealists used to do, ends up drawing attention to books that we would never otherwise have thought to read?

U. E. | The Surrealists weren't the only ones to advise against reading certain books or authors. That kind of polemical criticism has probably always existed.

J.-C. C. | André Breton created a list of authors that should and should not be read. Read Rimbaud, but not Verlaine. Read Hugo, but not Lamartine. Strangely: read Rabelais, but not Montaigne. If you were to follow his advice to the letter, you would probably miss out on some interesting books. Although I must say that

Breton did spare me from having to read *Le Grand Meaulnes,* for example.

U. E. | You haven't read *Le Grand Meaulnes*? You shouldn't have listened to Breton. It's a wonderful book.

J.-C. C. | It may not be too late. I know the Surrealists raged against Anatole France. But I read him anyway. And often enjoyed it – *The Revolt of the Angels*, for example. They were so vicious towards him. When he died, the Surrealists wanted to put his body into one of those long metal boxes used by the booksellers along the Seine, fill it up with the old books he so loved and throw it all into the river. Here too we sense a hatred for dusty, useless, annoying and often idiotic old books. Having said that, the question remains: are the books that have not been burned, badly recopied, poorly translated or censored, and have managed to make it to the present day, really the best of what has been written through the ages, and thus the books that we should read?

U. E. | We have talked about books that do not exist, or no longer exist. Books we haven't read that are waiting to be read, or will never be read. I would now like to talk about authors that do not exist, but that we have nevertheless heard of. Various publishing bigwigs were sitting round a table at the Frankfurt Book Fair. The top dogs of European publishing – Gaston Gallimard, Paul Flamand, Heinrich Ledig-Rowohlt and Valentino Bompiani. They were talking about the silly new publishing craze of overbidding on young authors who had not yet proved their worth. One of them came up with the idea of inventing an author. His name would be Milo Temesvar, author of the already acclaimed *Let Me Say Now*, for which the American Library had that very morning offered 50,000 dollars. They decided to spread the rumour and see what happened.

Bompiani returned to his stand and told my colleague and me, who were working for him at the time. We loved the idea, and started walking around the fair whispering about the soon-to-be-famous Milo Temesvar. During a dinner that evening, an ebullient Giangiacomo Feltrinelli came up to us and said, 'Don't waste your time. I've just bought the global rights to *Let Me Say Now*!' Milo Temesvar has been very important to me ever since. I once wrote an article reviewing one of his books, a parody of apocalyptic conspiracy theories called *The Patmos Sellers*. I described Milo Temesvar as an Albanian exiled from his country for being too left-wing, who had written a book inspired by Borges about the use of mirrors in chess. I even mentioned the obviously invented name of the publisher of the apocalypse book. I later found out that Arnoldo Mondadori – at the time the biggest name in Italian publishing – had cut out my article and scribbled 'Buy this book at any price' on it in red pen.

But that wasn't the end of Milo Temesvar. If you read the introduction to *The Name of the Rose*, you'll see that I mention one of his books. I've since found Temesvar referenced in various bibliographies. Recently I parodied *The Da Vinci Code* by referring to Temesvar's highly academic tomes on the books of Dan Brown, written in Georgian and Russian. So Milo Temesvar has been at my side throughout my life.

J.-P. DE T. | Well, the two of you have certainly absolved of guilt anyone with lots of books on their shelves that they've never read, and never will read.

J.-C. C. | It's important to clarify that a library is not necessarily made up of books that we've read, or even that we will eventually read. They should be books that we can read. Or that we may read. Even if we never do.

U. E. | A library is an assurance of learning.

J. P. DE T. | A bit like a wine cellar. There's no point in drinking it all.

J.-C. C. | I've actually built up a decent wine cellar too, and I know that I will leave some wonderful wine to my loved ones. Mainly because I drink less and less, and buy more and more. But I do know that if the desire should suddenly take me, I could go down to the cellar and polish off my best vintages. I buy wine *en primeur* – meaning that you pay for it the year it's harvested, and receive it three years later. The point being that, with a good Bordeaux for example, the producers keep it in barrels and then bottles in the best possible conditions. For those three years, your wine is improving and you haven't drunk it. It's an excellent system. By the time the three years are up, you've usually forgotten that you've bought it. You receive a present from yourself. It's wonderful!

J. P. DE T. | Shouldn't one do the same with books? Put them to one side – not necessarily in a cellar, but to allow them to ripen.

J.-C. C. | That would definitely offset the annoying 'novelty effect', in which we feel we should read something just

285

because it's new. Why not put aside a book that 'everyone is talking about', and read it three years later? I often do that with films. I don't have time to see everything I ought to see, so I put aside the films I'll get round to watching at some point. A little while later, both the need and the desire to watch almost all of them have passed. In that sense, buying *en primeur* is probably a filtering process in and of itself. I choose what I would like to drink in three years' time – or that's what I tell myself, anyway.

Another method is to have someone else – a more competent 'expert', who knows your taste – do the filtering for you. For years, I asked Gérard Oberlé to tell me what books I simply *had* to buy, regardless of my financial situation at the time. He would tell me, and I would obey. And that's how I bought *Pauliska or Modern Perversity: Recent Memoirs of a Young Polishwoman*, a late eighteenth-century novel that I have never come across again since that already long-ago time.

It contains a scene that I've always dreamed of adapting for the screen. One day a printer discovers that his wife has been unfaithful. The husband has proof, in the form of a letter his wife has received from her lover. So he sets the contents of the letter in type, undresses his wife, ties her to a table and prints the letter on her body, as deeply as he can. The naked, white body becomes paper, as the woman cries out in pain and becomes a book for evermore. It's a kind of a foreshadowing of Nathaniel Hawthorne's *The Scarlet Letter*. The fantasy of printing a letter on the body of a guilty woman has to be that of a printer, or possibly a writer.

Books on the altar and books in 'Hell'

J.-P. DE T. | We are paying a glowing tribute to the book, and to all books – those that have disappeared, those we haven't read and those we needn't read. This tribute must be understood within the context of cultures that consider the book sacred. Perhaps now is the time for you to say something about our 'religions of the Book'.

U. E. | It's important to note that it isn't quite accurate to call the three great monotheistic religions 'the religions of the Book', because Buddhism, Brahmanism and Confucianism also refer to books. The difference is that in monotheism the founding book takes on a particular meaning. It is revered because it is understood as some kind of translation or transcription of the divine word.

J.-C. C. | The Bible says, 'In the beginning was the Word, and the Word was with God, and the Word was God.' But how does the Word become writing? Why does the Book represent and incarnate the Word? How was that journey made, and with what guarantees? Because from those beginnings the simple fact of *writing* would take on an almost magical importance, as if those who possessed this supreme tool of being able to write thus enjoyed a secret bond with God and with the secrets

291

of Creation. Which brings us back to wondering what language the Word chose for its incarnation. If Christ had chosen the current time for his visit, he would definitely have spoken English. Or Chinese. But he spoke Aramaic, which was translated into Greek and then Latin. And of course each translation endangered the message. Did he really say what we suppose him to have said?

U. E. | An attempt to introduce the teaching of foreign languages into Texan schools in the nineteenth century was met by this sensible argument from the senator: 'Why should we need other languages, when English was good enough for Jesus?'

J.-C. C. | India is a completely different case. Books exist, of course, but the oral tradition remains of higher status, and is still considered more reliable. Why? Because the ancient texts were spoken, and especially sung, in groups. If someone made a mistake, the group would put him or her right. The oral tradition of the great epic poems, which has endured for almost a thousand years, is therefore likely to be more accurate than our transcriptions by monks copying out ancient texts by hand in their scriptoria, repeating the mistakes of their predecessors whilst adding their own. The notion of the word being divine, or even related to Creation, is not found in the Indian world – simply because the gods themselves were created. In the beginning there was a vast chaos, vibrating to musical movements and sounds. After millions of years, these sounds became vowels. Slowly, these vowels combined, became linked to consonants, transformed into words, and those words in turn combined to become the Vedas. The Vedas, therefore, have no author. They are the product of the cosmos, which is what gives them their authority. Who would dare question the word of the universe? But we can – and indeed must – attempt to understand it. The Vedas are extremely obscure, just like the infinite depths from which they sprang, so we need them to be explained by commentary – and thus we come to the Upanishads, the second category of Indian founding texts, and to the authors. This second category of texts and their authors gave birth to the gods. The words created the gods, rather than the other way round.

U. E. | It's no accident that the first linguists and grammarians were Indian.

J.-P. DE T. | Can you tell us how you were inducted into the 'religion of the Book'? What was your first contact with books?

J.-C. C. | I was born in the countryside, and there were no books in our house. As far as I know, my father read and reread the same book throughout his life. George Sand's *Valentine*. When people asked him why he kept rereading it, he would say, 'I'm very fond of it, so why read a different one?' My childhood books were the first books in the house, with the exception of a few old missals. The first book I remember seeing was the sacred book, at Mass; it had been placed in full view on the altar, and the priest turned the pages with great respect. My first book was therefore an object of worship. At the time, the priest used to turn his back on the congregation to read the Gospels passionately and with the opening words sung: '*In illo tempore, dixit Jesus discipulis suis . . .*'

Truth came out of a book, singing. Something very deep inside me considers the book as having a privileged, even sacred role to play; it still has pride of place on the altar of my childhood. The book, simply by being a book, contains a truth inaccessible to men.

Strangely enough, I came across that sentiment many years later, in a Laurel and Hardy film. I love Laurel and Hardy. Laurel is stating something, I can't remember what. Hardy is shocked, and asks him if he's sure. And Laurel replies, 'It's true, I read it in a book.' That argument is still good enough for me.

I became a bibliophile, if that's what I am, at a very young age. I still have a book list, eighty books long, that I wrote at the age of ten. Jules Verne, James Oliver Curwood, James Fenimore Cooper, Jack London, Thomas Mayne Reid and the rest. I've kept that list, as a kind of first catalogue. So there was always an attraction. It stemmed both from the lack of books and from the remarkable aura of the great missal in our rural area. It wasn't an antiphonary, but it was a very large book, and heavy for a child to carry.

U. E. | My initiation into books was very different. My paternal grandfather, who died when I was five or six, was a typographer. Like all typographers he was highly involved in the social and political struggles of his time. As a humanitarian socialist, he didn't just organise strikes with his friends, he invited the strike-breakers to lunch on strike days so they wouldn't get beaten!

We sometimes used to visit him at his home outside the city. Since retiring he had become a bookbinder. One of his bookshelves always held a stack of books waiting to be bound. Most of them were illustrated – you know, those popular nineteenth-century novels with plates by Joannot, Lenoir, etc . . . I'm sure my love of serialised novels was largely born then, from those visits to my grandfather's workshop. When he died, we found books at his place that he had been given to bind, but that no one had collected. They were all put into a huge box and inherited by my father, the eldest of thirteen sons.

That huge box then sat in the cellar of our family home, where I could fully indulge the curiosity awoken by my visits to my grandfather. I would be sent down to the cellar to collect coal to heat the house, or a bottle of wine, and would find myself among all these unbound books, which was an extraordinary thing for a child of eight. There was everything necessary to awaken my intelligence. Darwin, but also erotic books, and every episode – from 1912 to 1921 – of the *Giornale illustrato dei viaggi*, the Italian version of the *Journal des voyages et des aventures de terre et de mer*. My imagination was therefore fed by all those brave Frenchmen assailing vile Prussia, with me of course totally oblivious to the extreme nationalism of it all. Not to mention the incredible cruelty – the beheadings, the ruined virgins, the children disembowelled in exotic lands.

Sadly, this grandfatherly inheritance no longer exists. I read all the texts so many times, and lent them to so many friends, that they finally gave up the ghost. The Italian publisher Sonzogno used to specialise in those illustrated adventure stories. In the 1970s, the publishing group that published my work bought Sonzogno, and I was thrilled to think I might rediscover some of my childhood favourites, like *Les Ravageurs de la mer* by Louis Jacolliot, translated into Italian under the title *Il Capitano Satana*. But the publisher's collection had been hit by a bomb during the war. I've spent years rummaging through second-hand bookstalls and flea markets in an attempt to re-create my childhood library, but I still haven't found them all . . .

J.-C. C. | It's important to underline, as you have just done, quite how influential our childhood reading can be. Rimbaud scholars remind us how much *The Drunken Boat* owes to Gabriel Ferry's *Costal, the Indian Zapotec*. I notice, Umberto, that you started with adventure stories and serialised novels, and I with sacred books. Or a sacred book. Which might explain some of the differences between our journeys – who knows? The thing that really surprised me when I first visited India was that the Hindu religion doesn't have a book. There is no written text. The faithful are not given something to read or to sing, because most of them are illiterate.

That must be the reason why we in the West insist on talking about the 'religions of the Book'. The Hebrew Bible, the New Testament and the Koran are prestigious. They aren't meant for illiterates, for the uneducated and the lower classes. God may not have written them, but they are thought of as more or less dictated, or at least inspired, by Him. The Koran was dictated by an angel; the Prophet is asked to read (that's the very first order) and must admit that he cannot, that he has never learned. The gift of being able to read the Word, and therefore speak it, is then given to him. Religion and contact with God lift us up towards knowledge. One has to be able to read.

The Gospels were put together from the testimonies of the apostles, who had memorised the words of the Son of God. The Hebrew Bible depends on books. There are no other religions in which the book is the link between the divine world and the world of men. There are sacred Hindu texts, such as the Bhagavadgita. But again, they are not objects of religious worship as such.

J.-P. DE T. | Did the Greek and Roman civilisations worship the book?

U. E. | Not as a religious object.

J.-C. C. | The Romans may have venerated the Sibylline Books, which contained the oracles of Greek priestesses and were later burned by the Christians. For the Greeks, the two 'sacred' books were probably Hesiod and Homer. But one couldn't say that they are books of religious revelation.

U. E. | In polytheistic cultures, the idea of the revelation being 'authored' by a single person or being makes no sense, because no authority is considered superior to all others.

J.-C. C. | The Mahabharata was written by the bard Vyasa, who was the Indian equivalent of Homer. But this was before writing existed. Vyasa, the original author, didn't know how to write. He explains that he composed the 'great poem of the world', which tells us everything we need to know, but that he could not write it down, because he didn't know how. Men – or the gods – had not yet invented writing. Vyasa needed someone to write down what he knew, in order to establish truth among men thanks to the word. Brahma, therefore, sent him the deity Ganesh, with his little round belly, his elephant head and his writing case. When the time came to write, Ganesh broke off one of his tusks and dipped it in the ink. Which is why every picture shows him with a broken right tusk. And throughout the writing of the poem there was a creative rivalry between Ganesh and Vyasa. The Mahabharata is thus contemporaneous with the birth of writing. It is the first written work.

U. E. | They say that about the Homeric poems, too.

J.-C. C. | The veneration of the Gutenberg Bible that we've been talking about is completely justified in the context of our 'religions of the Book'. Modern book history starts with a Bible, too.

U. E. | But this veneration is mainly on the part of book collectors.

J.-C. C. | This sacredness of the book is testament to the importance that reading and writing have acquired and retained through successive civilisations. Without this sacred role, who could explain the power of the literate in China? Or of the scribes in ancient Egypt? Being able to read and write was the privilege of a minute group of individuals, and it gave them tremendous power. Imagine that you and I were the only two literate people around. We could enjoy mysterious exchanges and outrageous revelations in a private correspondence that no one could challenge.

J. P. DE T. | In his *A Universal History of the Destruction of Books*, Fernando Báez quotes John Chrysostom's work on the fourth-century custom of wearing old manuscripts around your neck to ward off evil.

J.-C. C. | Books have been thought of as talismans, but also as part of the black arts. The justification of the Spanish monks who burned the Mexican codices was that they were evil. Which is such a paradox. If the Spanish were protected by the strength of the one true God, how could the false gods have retained any kind of power? The same thing has been said of certain Tibetan books accused of containing fearsome esoteric teachings.

U. E. | Do you know of the work of Raimondo di Sangro (Prince of Sansevero) on 'quipus'?

J.-C. C. | Do you mean those knotted cords that the Inca Empire used in place of writing?

U. E. | Yes, exactly. In the eighteenth century, Madame de Graffigny wrote the hugely successful novel *Letters from a Peruvian Woman*. The Neapolitan prince and alchemist Raimondo di Sangro studied Mme de Graffigny's book in great depth and produced that wonderful illustrated book about quipus.

This Prince of Sansevero was a remarkable character. He was an occultist and most likely a Freemason as well, and is best known for decorating his chapel in Naples with sculptures of skinless human bodies with visible venous systems; the sculptures are so realistic that people have always thought he must have worked on living human bodies, perhaps the bodies of slaves he'd petrified by injecting them with various substances. If you ever visit Naples you absolutely must go and see them in the crypt of the Cappella Sansevero. His bodies are like three-dimensional renderings of Vesalius illustrations.

J.-C. C. | I'll be sure to go. But on the subject of the quipus, the remarkable interpretations they have engendered remind me of the massive land drawings in Peru, and people claiming that they were drawn to transmit messages to beings from outer space. Tristan Bernard wrote a short story on this theme: one day the people of Earth realise that they are being communicated with from outer space. They gather together to try and understand what these incomprehensible signals might be saying. They decide to draw enormous, 30-kilometre-high letters in the Sahara Desert to spell out the shortest possible phrase. They choose 'Like it?' It takes them years to write their enormous 'Like it?' in the sand. They are shocked, a little while later, to receive the reply, 'Thank you, but our message was not intended for you.'

This little deviation brings to mind a question I'd like to ask you, Umberto: what is a book? Is every object that involves readable characters a book? Were the Roman volumina books?

U. E. | Yes, they are considered part of book history.

J.-C. C. | The temptation is to say that any object that can be read is a book. But that's not true. A newspaper can be read but isn't a book, and the same goes for a letter, a gravestone, a banner in a demonstration, a label or my computer screen.

U. E. | It occurs to me that one way of defining what characterises a book is by considering the difference between a language and a dialect. Linguists have been unable to agree on this distinction. And yet we can illustrate it by saying that a dialect is a language without an army and navy. Venetian was considered a language because it was used in diplomatic and commercial affairs, which was never the case for the Piedmontese dialect.

J.-C. C. | So it remains a dialect.

U. E. | Quite. Therefore, if you have a little gravestone with just, for example, a name of God engraved on it, that isn't a book. But if it's an obelisk featuring several hieroglyphs telling the history of Egypt, then you have something resembling a book. It's the same distinction as between the text and the sentence. The sentence comes to an end wherever there's a full stop, whereas the text continues beyond the first full stop that punctuates the first sentence belonging to that text. 'I went home.' The sentence is over. 'I went home. My mother was there.' Already, we're in the realm of textuality.

J.-C. C. | I'd like to quote from Paul Claudel's 1925 essay on the philosophy of the book, taken from a lecture given in Florence. I'm no great fan of Claudel's work, but he did have a few amazing insights. He starts with a mystical declaration: 'We know that the world is in effect a text, and that it speaks to us, humbly and joyfully, of its own absence but also of the eternal presence of someone else, namely its creator.'

Now, these could only be the words of a Christian. A little later he writes: 'I have decided to study the physiology of the book – the word, the page and the book. The word is nothing but an untamed part of the sentence, a small stretch of the path towards sense, the giddy glimpse of a passing idea. The Chinese word, on the other hand, stands complete in front of us . . . The mysterious thing about writing is that it speaks to us. Both ancient and modern Latin were always intended to be written on stone. The first books have an architectural beauty. Then, as the brain started to move faster, the flood of thought-matter became more dense, the lines narrower, the writing rounder and shorter. Before long the printed word had taken over and standardised the wet and shimmering layer left by the cramped nib of the pen . . . Human writing became stylised, simplified into something mechanical . . . The verse is a line which stops not because it has arrived at a physical boundary and space is lacking, but because its internal code has been achieved and its power used up . . . The pages appear to us one after the other like the successive terraces of a large garden. The eye delights at the almost sideways attack of an adjective suddenly released into the neuter noun with the fierceness of dark red, or fire . . . A great library always reminds me of the stratifications of a coalmine – full of fossils, tracks and stories. It's the herbarium of feelings and passions, the jar in which the dried-up fragments of all human societies are stored.'

U.E. | That is a perfect illustration of the difference between poetry and rhetoric. Poetry would give you a fresh perspective on writing, books and libraries. Claudel, on the other hand, tells us exactly what we already know. The verse doesn't end because it reaches the end of the page, but because it is obeying an internal rule, etc. It may be sublime rhetoric, but he doesn't give us a single new idea.

J.-C. C. | Where Claudel sees 'the stratifications of a coalmine' in his library, a friend of mine compares his books to a warm fur coat. He feels warmed and sheltered by his books; protected against error, uncertainty and also wintry weather. It is very comforting to be surrounded by all the ideas in the world, all the feelings, all the knowledge and every possible wrong turning. You'll never be cold with your books around you. You will at the very least be protected against the icy threats of ignorance.

U. E. | The atmosphere of the library itself is also part of creating this sense of protectedness. The structure should preferably be old – that is, made of wood. The lamps should be just like the green ones in the Bibliothèque nationale. The juxtaposition of brown and green helps create that particular atmosphere. The very modern (and in its way perfectly nice) Toronto Library doesn't engender the same feeling of being protected as Yale's Sterling Memorial Library, with its faux-Gothic style and different storeys with their nineteenth-century furnishings. It was actually in Yale's Sterling Library that I had the idea for the murder in the library in *The Name of the Rose*. I used to work there in the evenings, on the mezzanine floor, and it felt as if anything could happen. There wasn't a lift up to the mezzanine, so you felt that once you were sitting at your table working, nobody would be able to come to your assistance. Your corpse might be found days after the crime, stuffed under a bookshelf. The place had that preserved feeling you get around graves and memorial monuments.

J.-C. C. | What I've always loved about those big public libraries is the little rim of green light surrounding the white light shining down on one's book. You have your book, and you're surrounded by the books of the world. The detail and the overview. That's why I never go into those cold, anonymous modern libraries, where the books aren't on display. We have totally forgotten that libraries can be beautiful.

U. E. | When I was writing my thesis, I spent a lot of time in the Saint-Geneviève Library in Paris. It was easy, in those kinds of libraries, to focus on the books that did indeed surround you, and to take notes from them. Once the Rank Xerox photocopiers turned up, it was the beginning of the end. You could copy the book and take it home with you. Your house became filled with photocopies. And the fact of having them at home meant that you didn't bother reading them.

It's the same with the Internet. Either you print things out, and find yourself oppressed by piles of documents you'll never read, or you read online, but as soon as you click onto the next page you forget what you've just read, the very thing that has brought you to the page now on your screen.

J.-C.C. | Here's something we haven't yet discussed: how do we decide which books to put next to each other? Why do we arrange our books in this or that order? Why might we sometimes change the way our library is organised? Is it simply so that the books can rub shoulders with new books? So they can make new friends? Have new neighbours? I feel sure that there is a relationship between them – I hope so, and I encourage it. I move those at the bottom up to eye level to restore a little of their dignity, to reassure them that I didn't think they were somehow inferior, and thus contemptible and deserving of the bottom shelf.

We've already talked about this. Of course we have to filter, or at least help with the inevitable filtering, and of course we have to try to save the books that according to us mustn't be lost in the process; the books that might please those who come after us, or help them, or amuse them at our expense. We also have to create meaning, carefully and to the extent that we can. But we are living in difficult, uncertain times, and the priority for each of us must be to encourage exchanges of knowledge, experience, perspective, hopes and actions. And to compare each with each. That will perhaps be the first task of the next generation. Lévi-Strauss said that cultures are only alive to the extent that they are in contact with other cultures. A solitary culture is no culture at all.

308

U. E. | My secretary once wanted to draw up a catalogue of my books so that she knew exactly where each one was. I persuaded her not to. While I was writing *The Search for the Perfect Language* I looked at my library anew, with new criteria, and changed it around. Which books would best nourish my thoughts on the subject? When I finished writing, some books went back on the linguistics shelf, and some to aesthetics, but others were already being used for a new piece of research.

J.-C. C. | There's nothing more difficult than organising a library. Apart from trying to organise the world, that is. Who would try? How are you going to do it? By subject? But then you'll have books of very different sizes, and might have trouble with the shelf heights. By format, then? Era? Author? Some authors write on all kinds of subjects. If you classified by subject, you'd have books by someone like Kircher on every shelf.

U. E. | Leibniz struggled with the same thing. For him, it was about organising a body of knowledge. As it was for Diderot and D'Alembert with their *Encyclopédie*.

J.-C. C. | This only became a serious problem quite recently. In the seventeenth century, a large private library would have contained no more than 3,000 books.

U. E. | For the simple reason that, as we have said, books were hugely more expensive then. A manuscript cost a fortune. To the extent that it was sometimes preferable to copy it out by hand than to buy it.

I'd like to tell you a funny story. I once went to the Coimbra Library, in Portugal. The tables were covered with felt blankets, rather like billiard tables. I asked why. They told me that it was to protect the books from bat droppings. Why not get rid of the bats? Because they ate the worms that attacked the books. But the worm too must not be completely banned or eliminated. The worm's journey through the incunabulum allows us to see how the sheets were bound together, and whether some bits are newer than others. And the worm-tracks sometimes form interesting patterns that add character to the ancient books. Book-collecting manuals are full of instructions about protecting your books from worms. One resource is Zyklon B, which the Nazis used in their gas chambers. It is, of course, better used to kill insects than men, but it does still seem rather creepy.

A less barbaric technique is to keep an alarm clock in your library. The kind our grandmothers used to have. Apparently the regular tick-tock, and the vibrations it sends through the wood, keep the worms in their hidey-holes.

J.-C. C. | An alarm clock that sends them to sleep, one might say.

J.-P. DE T. | The context of our 'religions of the Book' definitely creates a strong incentive to read. And yet the great majority of humans live a long way from libraries and bookshops. For them, the book is irrelevant.

U. E. | A London study found that a quarter of the people surveyed thought that Winston Churchill and Charles Dickens were imaginary characters, whereas Robin Hood and Sherlock Holmes had really existed.

J.-C. C. | Ignorance is all around us, and often arrogant and proud. Evangelical, even. Sure of itself, declaiming its triumphs through the narrow mouths of our politicians. Whereas fragile, changing, self-doubting, constantly threatened erudition seems one of the final bastions of a more utopian vision. Do you really think it's important to be well educated?

U. E. | I think it's fundamental.

J.-C. C. | That the greatest number of people know the greatest number of things possible?

U. E. | That the greatest number of us are educated about the past. Yes. That's the basis of every civilisation. The old man telling his tribe's stories under the oak tree is establishing that tribe's link with the past, and passing down the learning accumulated over the years. The current generation is probably tempted to think, as the Americans do, that what happened 300 years ago no longer matters, that it's irrelevant. George W. Bush hadn't read about how the English fought wars in Afghanistan, so he couldn't learn from their experiences, and sent his troops off to the slaughter. If Hitler had studied Napoleon's Russian campaign, he wouldn't have been so stupid as to throw his troops into battle there. He would have known that the summer is never long enough to arrive in Moscow before winter.

J.-C. C. | We've discussed those who try to ban books, and those who don't read out of ignorance or sheer laziness. But what about Nicholas of Cusa's theory of 'learned ignorance'? St Bernard wrote to the Abbot of Vauclair, Henri Murdach, that 'one can learn more from a tree leaf than from any book . . . the trees and the rocks will teach you things you could not learn from any teacher'. The very fact that it contains a text that has been articulated and printed means a book has nothing to teach us, and is in fact suspect, because it seeks to spread the ideas of a single individual. Real wisdom is to be found in the contemplation of nature. I don't know if you're familiar with José Bergamin's wonderful essay on illiteracy? He asks what we have lost in learning to read. What kinds of knowledge did prehistoric peoples (or any illiterate peoples) possess that we have irredeemably lost ? Like all good questions, there is no simple answer.

U.E. | It seems to me that each of us can answer for ourselves. The great mystics had various responses to the question. For example in his *The Imitation of Christ,* Thomas à Kempis said that he had never been able to find peace in his life except in being alone somewhere with a book. Jakob Böhme, on the contrary, had his great epiphany when a ray of light struck the pewter dish in front of him. He didn't care whether or not he had a book to hand, because the entire purpose of his life was revealed to him in that instant. But we book people wouldn't know what to do with a ray of light on a dish.

J.-C.C. | This brings me back to our libraries. Perhaps you've had an experience like this: I often walk into one of the rooms where I keep my books simply to look at them, without touching a single one. It feeds me in a way I cannot explain. It feeds my curiosity and at the same time reassures me. When I was running the French film school, I heard that Jean-Luc Godard was looking for a place to work in Paris. We let him squat in one of our rooms, on the condition that he let a few students sit in when he edited his films. So he shot a film and, once the shoot was over, put all the different-coloured boxes that contained the different sequences on the bookshelves. Before starting the edit he spent days just looking at the rolls of film, without opening them. It wasn't a performance. He was on his own. Just looking at the boxes. I used to pop by to see him from time to time. And there he would be, trying to remember, perhaps, or looking for inspiration, for a narrative.

U. E. | That experience isn't only for people who own lots of books, or rolls of film, as in your example. It can happen in a public library, or even a large bookshop. Which of us hasn't drawn sustenance from the simple smell of the books on the shelves, despite them not belonging to us. Gazing at books in the hope of extracting knowledge. All those books you haven't read and that are so full of promise. One reason to be cheerful is that more and more people now have the opportunity to gaze at great quantities of books. When I was a child, bookshops were severe, unwelcoming places. You walked in and a man dressed in black would ask you what you wanted. He was so frightening that it wouldn't occur to you to linger. We are living in the first era in any civilisation to have so many bookshops, so many beautiful, light-filled bookshops to wander around in, flicking through books, discovering new treasures on three or four storeys – as in the Fnac bookshops in France, or Feltrinelli in Italy. When I go there I notice that they are full of young people. As I've said, they don't need to buy the books, or even read them. It's enough just to flick through, and glance at the back cover. We too have learned many things from reading mere summaries. One might protest that among six billion humans on the planet, there are still very few who read. But when I was a kid there were only two billion of us on the planet and the bookshops were deserted. It seems to me that the percentage has improved.

J.-P. DE T. | And yet you have said that the abundance of data on the Internet risks producing six billion separate encyclopaedias, and thus being utterly counter-productive, and actually paralysing . . .

U. E. | There's a difference between the 'moderate' overwhelm of a great bookshop and the infinite overwhelm of the Internet.

J.-P. DE T. | We've been talking about the 'religions of the Book' and how they make the book into a sacred object. The Book then becomes the ultimate reference, disqualifying and prohibiting any book that diverges from the values it conveys. It seems to me that this is the time to discuss the places in our libraries where forbidden books are stored – not burned, perhaps, but kept hidden so as to protect the sensibilities of potential readers. Like the (largely pornographic) books that were placed in what was called the *'Enfer'*, the Hell, of the Bibliothèque nationale.

J.-C. C. | There are various ways of approaching this. For example, I was shocked to find out that in the whole of Spanish literature there wasn't a single erotic text published before the second half of the twentieth century. That's a kind of *'Enfer'* in itself.

U. E. | The Spanish are, however, authors of the world's worst blasphemy – so bad that I wouldn't dare quote it here.

J.-C. C. | Yes – but not a single erotic text. A Spanish friend told me that when he was a kid, in the Sixties and Seventies, a friend showed him a mention of *tetas* – women's nipples – in *Don Quixote*. In the 1960s and

'70s, a young Spanish boy could still be shocked and even aroused by finding the word *tetas* in Cervantes. Apart from that, nothing. Not even barrack-room songs. Every great French author from Rabelais to Apollinaire has written at least one pornographic text. But not the Spanish. In Spain, the Inquisition actually succeeded in getting rid of the vocabulary – stifling the words, if not the deeds. Even Ovid's *The Art of Love* was banned for a long time. It's even more bizarre when you think that some of the Latin authors who wrote this kind of literature had Spanish roots – I'm thinking of Martial, for example, who came from Calatayud.

U. E. | Other civilisations were much freer about sex, as we can see from some of the Pompeii frescos and Indian sculptures. The Renaissance was fairly liberal, but then during the Counter-Reformation they started painting clothes onto Michelangelo's nudes. The situation in the Middle Ages was even more interesting – the official art was exceedingly prudish and pious, but folklore and the Goliard poems were bursting with obscenity . . .

J.-C. C. | People say that the Indians invented eroticism, perhaps simply because the *Kama Sutra* is the earliest known guide to sex. And it does in fact show every possible position and every kind of sexuality, as do the carvings at the Khajuraho temples. But since that apparently voluptuous time, India has become more and more puritanical. In contemporary Indian cinema they don't even kiss on the mouth. This can be explained by the influence of Islam on the one hand, and the English Victorians on the other. Having said that, I'm not convinced that there isn't also an authentically Indian puritanism. Moving on to recent history in our part of the world, let me go back to my student days in the 1950s. I remember having to go down to the basement of a bookshop on the boulevard de Clichy, on the corner of rue Germain-Pilon, to find erotic books. Barely fifty-five years ago. So we don't have much to brag about, either!

U. E. | But then that was exactly the idea behind the '*Enfer*' collection at Paris' Bibliothèque nationale. It wasn't about banning those books, but about keeping them out of reach of the general public.

J.-C. C. | The Bibliothèque nationale's '*Enfer*' collection is basically made up of pornographic-type books that went against contemporary standards of decency. It was created just after the Revolution with books confiscated from monasteries, castles, the occasional private collection and also the royal library. The name '*l'Enfer*' was conferred upon it during the Restoration, a time of renewed conservatism of every kind. I like the fact that you need special permission to visit book-Hell. We think it's easy to go to Hell. But no. Hell is locked away; not just anyone can get in. Having said that, the library did organise an exhibition of these books brought out of Hell, and it was very successful.

J.-P. DE T. | Have you visited that Hell?

U. E. | What is the point, given that all the books it contains have now been published anyway?

J.-C. C. | I only saw a small part of the exhibition. I'm sure it does contain books that you and I have read, but in very rare collectors' editions. And it's not only a collection of French books. There's a rich tradition of Arabic literature on the subject. There are *Kama Sutra* equivalents in Arabic and also Persian. And yet, just as we were saying about India, the Arab-Muslim world seems to have forgotten its outrageous beginnings in favour of an unexpected puritanism that runs quite contrary to local tradition.

But let's return to France in the eighteenth century. That was definitely the era when illustrated erotic literature, which seems to have originated in Italy two centuries earlier, appeared and became popular, albeit published clandestinely. Sade, Mirabeau and Restif de la Bretonne were sold under the table. These authors were writing pornographic books telling variations on more or less the same story, of a young woman arriving in Paris from the countryside and finding herself prey to all the debaucheries of the capital.

This was actually pre-revolutionary literature in disguise. At the time, eroticism in literature seriously disturbed public decency and righteousness. It was perceived as a direct attack on decorum. People feared that guns were lurking behind the orgiastic scenes. Mirabeau is one of these erotic writers; for him, sex is social upheaval. This relationship between eroticism, pornography and a pre-revolutionary society obviously no longer existed after the revolutionary period itself. One mustn't forget that during the Terror the real enthusiasts in this regard used to rent a carriage, go to the place de la Concorde to watch a major execution, and then – at great danger to themselves – make a day of it with some fun and frolics in the carriage, or in the square itself.

The Marquis de Sade, a matchless phenomenon in the field, was a revolutionary. He was imprisoned for his behaviour, rather than his writings. So it's important to emphasise that those books of his really were extremely hot to the touch. The reading as well as the writing of those fiery lines was a subversive act.

This subversive dimension of erotic writing continued after the Revolution, but in the social rather than the political sphere. Not, of course, that this prevented books from being banned. Which is why some authors of pornographic novels have always denied having written them, right up to the present day. Aragon always denied having written *Irene's Cunt*. But one thing is for sure – they didn't write these books to make money.

The ban on these books destined for Hell meant that very few copies were sold. It was more a need to write than a desire to make money. When Musset wrote *Gamiani* with George Sand, he was probably just desperate to escape his usual sentimentality. Which he certainly did, giving us 'two nights of excess'.

I have often discussed these issues with Milan Kundera. He thinks that Christianity has managed to reach right into lovers' beds, making them feel guilty during their erotic games, and as if they have sinned – which might be rather delicious while indulging in, for example, anal sex, but afterwards has to be confessed and atoned for. The sin, therefore, brings one back to the Church. Whereas communism never achieved that. Marxism–Leninism may have been complex and powerful, but it stopped on the threshold of the bedroom. In Prague under the communist dictatorship, a couple making love illicitly would still have a sense of doing something subversive. They might lack freedom in every aspect and act of their lives, but not in bed.

What will happen to your book collections when you die?

J.-P. DE T. | Jean-Claude, you've told us that you weren't too distressed when you once had to sell part of your book collection. I would now like to ask you both what will become of these collections of yours. Anyone who has created a collection, a labour of love, clearly has to think about what will happen when he is no longer in a position to look after it. I would therefore like, if you don't mind, to talk about the fate of your collections after you pass away.

J.-C. C. | My collection was indeed amputated, and oddly it caused me no pain at all to sell a whole bundle of beautiful books. Although a lovely, surprising thing also happened as a result.

I had given Gérard Oberlé part of my Surrealist collection – which included some precious manuscripts and signed books – and asked him to sell it off bit by bit. The day I finally cleared my debts, I phoned him to ask what had been sold. He told me that quite a few hadn't yet found buyers, and I asked him to return them. It was more than four years later, and my memory of these books had started to fade. I rediscovered them with as much delight as when I had first bought them. Like great bottles of wine I'd thought I'd already drunk.

What will happen to my books when I die? My
wife and two daughters will decide. In my will I shall
probably leave particular books to particular friends.
A kind of posthumous present, a sign, a handover. So
that they don't forget me entirely. I'm just pondering
what I would like to leave you. If only I had a Kircher
you don't have . . . But no such luck.

U. E. | I obviously wouldn't want my collection to be
dispersed. My family could give it to a public library,
or else sell it through an auction house, which would
mean the collection would go to a university intact.
That's all I care about.

J.-C. C. | Yours is a real collection. It's a work of art that
you've put a lot of effort into creating, so of course
you don't want it broken up. It possibly says as much
about you as the books you've written. I would say the
same thing in my own case: the eclecticism that has
led to the creation of my library also says a great deal
about me. People have always told me that I spread
myself too thin. So my library is the perfect reflection.

U. E. | I don't know if mine is an accurate reflection of me.
As I've said, I collect books whose contents I don't
believe, so it must be more like a mirror image. Or

perhaps a reflection of my contradictory nature. I'm not sure, because I don't show my collection to many people. A book collection is a solitary, masturbatory kind of phenomenon, and you don't often come across people who share your passions. If you own beautiful paintings, people come over to admire them. But no one is sincerely interested in your collection of old books. They don't understand why you're so attached to some ugly little old book, or how you could have spent years tracking it down.

J.-C. C. | I would justify our naughty habit by saying that possessing an original book is almost like having a direct relationship with the author. A book collection can be thought of as a gathering, a group of living friends, a collection of people. You can go to them whenever you feel a bit lonely or depressed. They are there for you. And sometimes I rummage through them and find hidden treasures I had forgotten existed.

U. E. | As I said, it's a solitary vice. I don't know why, but the attachment one can have to a book has nothing to do with its commercial value. I am deeply attached to several books that are not worth much at all.

J.-P. DE T. | How large are your collections?

U. E. | I think people often confuse a collection of books that one owns with a collection of ancient books. I have 50,000 books in my various homes. But these are modern books. I also have 1,200 rare titles. There's another difference, too. The ancient books are books I have chosen and paid for, whereas the modern ones are made up not only of the books I have bought over the years, but also, and increasingly, those that people have sent me as tributes. I give lots of them to my students, but I do keep a fair few, and that's how I've got to 50,000.

J.-C. C. | Not counting my collection of legends and fairy tales, I own perhaps 2,000 ancient books, out of a total of 30,000 or 40,000. But some of the new ones can be a bit of a burden. It's hard to get rid of a book that a friend has signed, for example. That friend might come to visit, and he has to see his book – and in prime position, too.

Some people cut out the message on the title page so they can sell their books at the second-hand book-stalls along the Seine. That's almost as bad as cutting up incunabula to sell them page by page. I imagine that you must also receive lots of books from Umberto Eco's many friends around the world.

328

U. E. | I once did some calculations about this. It was quite a while ago, and I should probably do it again. I researched the price per square metre of a Milan apartment that was neither in the old town (too expensive) nor in the poor suburbs. I had to get my head around the fact that a nice, reasonably bourgeois apartment would cost me 6,000 euros per square metre, or 300,000 for an apartment of fifty square metres. I then subtracted the doors, windows and other elements that cut down on the apartment's 'vertical' space (namely the walls that might host bookshelves), and that left me with only twenty-five square metres. So one vertical square metre would cost me 12,000 euros.

I then researched the cheapest price for a six-shelf bookcase, which was 500 euros per square metre. I could probably store about 300 books in a six-shelf square metre. The cost of storing each book would therefore be about 42 euros. More than the price of the book itself. So each person who sent me a book should include a cheque for that amount. And much more, if it was a large-format art book.

J.-C. C. | It's the same with translations. What are you supposed to do with the five copies of your book sent to you by the Burmese publisher? You tell yourself that you'll give them to any Burmese you happen to meet. But you'd have to meet five!

329

U. E. | I've a whole cellar full of translations of my work. I tried sending them to prisons. I was sure that there'd be fewer Americans, French and Germans in Italian prisons than Albanians and Croats, so I sent the translations in the latter languages.

J.-C. C. | How many languages was *The Name of the Rose* translated into?

U. E. | Forty-five. The number is partly a result of the fall of the Berlin Wall: whereas beforehand Russian was the compulsory language in all Soviet republics, afterwards the book had to be translated into Ukrainian, Azerbaijani etc. Hence the outrageous number. Given that one receives five to ten copies of each translation, that's 225–450 books sitting in my cellar.

J.-C. C. | Let me tell you a secret: I sometimes throw them out, while trying to fool myself that I'm not.

U. E. | I once agreed to be on the jury for the Viareggio book prize, as a favour to its president. I was only on the non-fiction panel, but I soon realised that every member of the jury received all the books submitted, for all the categories. For the poetry section alone – and you know as well as I do that the world is full of poets self-publishing their marvellous verse – I received whole crates of books I had no idea what to do with. Then there were all the other categories. I presumed I was supposed to keep all of it as evidence. But I soon ran out of space and, thank God, gave up my place on the jury. The haemorrhage stopped. The poets are by far the most dangerous.

J.-C. C. | Do you know that joke about Argentina, land of many poets? One of these poets bumps into an old friend, reaches into his pocket and says, 'Oh, great timing, I've just finished a poem, let me read it to you.' The other man puts his hand into his own pocket and says, 'Watch out, I've got one too!'

U. E. | But doesn't Argentina have even more psychoanalysts than poets?

J.-C. C. | Apparently so. Although the two aren't mutually exclusive.

U. E. | My collection of ancient books is nothing compared to the Dutch bibliophile Joost Ritman's Bibliotheca Philosophica Hermetica. Having collected almost every important book on the Hermetic traditions, he recently started collecting precious incunabula on other subjects, too. The library's modern books cover the whole top floor of a large building, whereas the incunabula are kept in a beautifully converted cellar.

J.-C. C. | The Brazilian collector José Mindlin had a whole house built for his unique collection of so-called Americana. He has also created a foundation that will enable the Brazilian government to maintain this library after his death. On a much more modest level, I have two little collections for which I would like to ensure a decent fate. One of them is, I think, totally unique. It's a collection of the founding myths, legends and fairy tales of every country. It isn't a collection of precious books in the way that a book collector might think of the word. The tales are anonymous, the editions are often cheap and the copies sometimes worn. I would like to leave this collection of 3,000 or 4,000 books to a museum of popular arts, or a specialist library. I haven't yet found the right place.

The second collection for which I would like – and haven't yet been able – to find the right home is the one my wife and I have built. As I've already said, it concerns 'Persian Journeys' since the sixteenth century. Perhaps our daughter will take an interest at some point.

U. E. | My children don't seem to. My son likes the fact that I own a first edition of Joyce's *Ulysses,* and my daughter often consults my Mattioli Herbarium from the sixteenth century, but that's about it. Having said that, I only became a true book lover around the age of fifty.

J.-P. DE T. | Does either of you worry about theft?

J.-C. C. | Someone once stole a book from me, and not any old book – a first edition of Sade's *Philosophy in the Bedroom*. I think I know who took it. It was when I was moving house. I've never been able to get it back.

U. E. | It must have been someone who knew what they were doing. The greatest threat is from book-loving thieves, who take only one book. Booksellers soon spot these kleptomaniac customers, and point them out to their colleagues. Your average type of thief isn't too much of a problem for the collector. Imagine some poor housebreaker deciding to steal my collection. It would take them two nights to box up all the books, and they'd need a lorry to transport them.

Then unscrupulous (because it would be obvious that they were stolen goods) booksellers would buy them for next to nothing. Unless of course the entire lot was bought by gentleman-thief Arsène Lupin and hidden in the Hollow Needle. In any case, proper collectors create files for each of their rare books, listing any defects or other identifying marks, and there is also a specialist police department dealing with art and book theft. The Italian one is particularly effective, having learned its trade recovering art works lost during the war. Finally, if the burglar did decide to take only three books, he would be bound to think that the biggest or most beautifully bound books were the most valuable and take them, whereas the most precious book may actually be so small that it passes unnoticed.

The major risk is the person sent specially by a mad collector who knows that you possess a certain book and will stop at nothing, even theft, to get their hands on it. But that kind of risk would only be worth it for the 1623 Shakespeare Folio.

J.-C. C. | Did you know that there are 'antiques dealers' who produce catalogues of antique furniture still at its owner's house. If you want it, they will organise the theft of that single piece. But in general, I agree with what you've been saying. I was burgled once. The burglars took the TV, a radio and some other stuff I can't remember, but not a single book. The value of what they took was about 10,00 euros, whereas they could have taken a single book worth five or ten times that amount. Meaning that we are protected by people's ignorance.

334

J.-P. DE T. | I imagine that every book collector is to some extent haunted by the fear of fire?

U. E. | Oh yes! That's why I pay a substantial premium to insure my collection. It's no accident that I wrote a book about a library burning down. I'm always worrying about it happening to my house. And I've found out why. The head fireman of our town lived in the apartment above us, from when I was three to when I was ten. There would often – sometimes several times a week – be a fire in the middle of the night and the firemen would arrive, sirens blaring, to get their boss out of bed. I would wake up to the sound of his boots running down the stairs. The next day, his wife would tell my mother all the gory details . . . So you can see why my childhood was haunted by the threat of fire.

J.-P. DE T. | I would like to come back to the fate of your patiently built collections . . .

J.-C. C. | I can imagine that my wife and daughters might sell all or part of my collection to pay the inheritance tax, or something like that. I don't find the thought sad – quite the opposite: when ancient books come back on the market they can once again scatter, travel, make people happy, nourish the passion for books. You probably remember the rich American collector Colonel Sickels, who possessed the greatest imaginable collection of nineteenth- and twentieth-century French literature. He sold his collection through the Drouot auction house while he was still alive. The sale lasted two weeks. I met him shortly afterwards. He had no regrets. He was even proud to have impassioned a few hundred genuine enthusiasts for a couple of weeks.

U. E. | The subject of my collection is so eccentric that I'm not sure whom exactly it would interest. I wouldn't like my books to end up in the hands of an occultist; they would of course value them, but for different reasons. Perhaps the Chinese would buy my collection? I once received an issue of *Semiotica,* a journal produced in the United States. It was dedicated to semiotics in China, and it cited my works more often that our specialist publications do. Perhaps one day the real interest in my collection will come from Chinese researchers seeking to understand all the follies of the West.